The illustrated book of
Card Games
for One

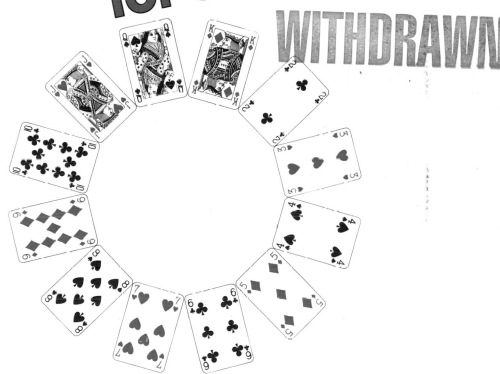

The illustrated book of

Card Games
for One

Over 120 games of Solitaire

George F. Hervey

Illustrated by Karel Feuerstein

CHARTWELL
BOOKS INC.

Contents

The publishers wish to thank Waddingtons Playing Card Co Ltd for supplying the playing cards used in the illustrations

Published by
Chartwell Books Inc.
A Division of Book Sales Inc.
110 Enterprise Avenue
Secaucus
New Jersey 07094

Originally published in Great Britain by
The Hamlyn Publishing Group Limited
Feltham, Middlesex
Copyright © The Hamlyn Publishing Group Limited 1977

ISBN 0–89009–113–7

Library of Congress Catalog Card Number: 76-52565

Typeset in England
by Filmtype Services Limited, Scarborough
Printed in England
by Hazell Watson & Viney Limited, Aylesbury

795
9 H
1977

Introduction

Some card players have been heard to say that a game of patience is a waste of time. (In the U.S.A. a patience game is more usually known as solitaire. It may be a more descriptive name, but I have retained the English name because, in the U.K., solitaire has been appropriated by a game that is played with marbles on a board.) In fact it is not. It has many virtues, not the least being that it teaches one the self-discipline of being honest with oneself.

No-one knows, and probably no-one ever will, how games of patience arose. The first known use of playing cards (tarot pack) was divination; and it is easy to suggest that patience games grew out of the dealing and selecting of the pictorial lay-outs of the fortune tellers, and that the more advanced games for two, three, and more, players were, in turn, developed out of patience games. In reality, however, this is mere conjecture with no concrete evidence to support it.

In England the first book about patience games was published *circa* 1870. Entitled *Illustrated Games of Patience* it was the work of Lady Adelaide Cadogan, daughter of the 1st Marquess of Anglesey and wife of the youngest son of the 3rd Earl of Cadogan. She describes 24 games. In the intervening century many more have been invented, and many books describing them written.

From them the present writer has extracted a selection of games chosen so there should be food for every taste. Some he found long-winded to the point of confusion, and his two chief sources were *The Complete Patience Book* (1948) by Basil Dalton with its donnish wit, and the well-presented and well-written *Complete Book of Patience* (1950) by Albert Morehead and Geoffrey Mott-Smith. To them he is much indebted. If some who read this book find the description of a game less adequate than they would wish, they are reminded that he who plays a game of patience is not subject to a strict code of laws laid down by a governing body but only to the general principle described in the text. It is for the individual player to determine the details for himself.

Games of patience fall into two main groups: those played with one pack of cards (single-pack games) and those played with two packs (double-pack games) shuffled together. This well-defined division has been retained in the text (games played with less than one pack are treated as single-pack games) and within the groups the games are arranged in alphabetical order. It is not an ideal arrangement, but it is a convenient one and it has the advantage, in these inflationary days, that the contents page also serves as an index. Patience games that are played with three and even four packs of cards are excluded. They are very cumbersome, even when played with the extra-small packs made for patience games, and the inventors of these games seem to think that ingenious irritation is a fair exchange for inviting interest. I am not so sure.

George F. Hervey,
Bagshot, Surrey, England
1977

Single-pack Games

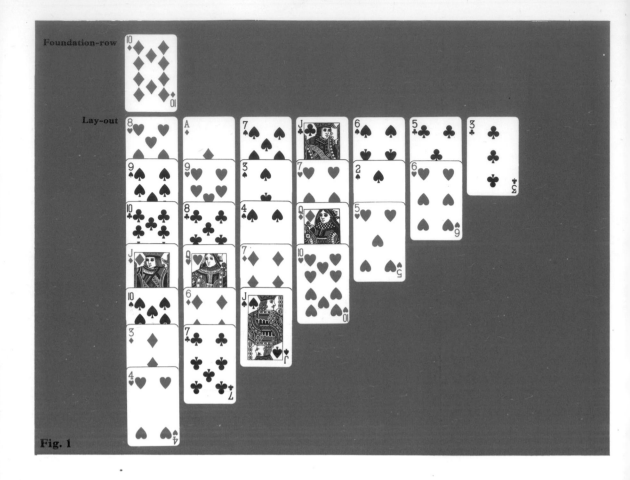

Fig. 1

Agnes

Deal face upwards to the board 28 cards in a row of seven cards, one of six cards, and so, dealing one card less each time, to a row of one card, if one card can be said to make a row. For convenience the rows may overlap. The twenty-ninth card is dealt face upwards to the centre as a foundation-card, and, as they become available, the other three cards of the same rank will be placed in line with it (*see* Fig. 1).

The object of the game is to build on the foundation-cards ascending, round-the-corner suit sequences.

The bottom card of a column in the lay-out is exposed. It may be built on a foundation, packed on an exposed card in the lay-out, or itself be packed on, in a descending sequence of the same colour (not necessarily of the same suit). A sequence may be moved from one column to another only as a whole and only if all the cards of the sequence are of the same suit. If a vacancy occurs by reason of all the cards of a column being moved, it may, not necessarily must, be filled

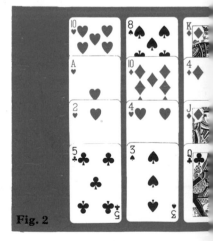

Fig. 2

10

Fig. 1 Agnes

Play the 10 ♥ to the foundation-row.

Pack the 5 ♥ on the 6 ♥ and the 4 ♥ on the 5 ♥.

Pack the 2 ♠ on the 3 ♣, and the 6 ♠ on the 7 ♣.

Move the Q ♦ into the vacancy, and pack the 6 ♥, 5 ♥ and 4 ♥ together on the 7 ♥.

Pack the 5 ♣ on the 6 ♠ and move the 7 ♥, 6 ♥, 5 ♥ and 4 ♥ together into the vacancy.

And so on.

Fig. 2 Baker's Dozen

The 3 ♥ is packed on the 4 ♣, the A ♠ is played to the centre and the 2 ♠ built on it.

The 6 ♠ is packed on the 7 ♠, the A ♣ is played to the centre and the 2 ♣ built on it.

The 4 ♠ is packed on the 5 ♣, the A ♦ is played to the centre and the 2 ♦ and 3 ♦ built on it.

And so on.

with any available card, or sequence of cards that are all of the same suit.

After all possible moves have been made, a card is dealt face upwards to the bottom of each column, and the game continues until the stock is exhausted.

After the third deal has been made from the stock, there will be two cards left in hand. They are available for play either to a foundation or to the lay-out.

Baker's Dozen

Deal the complete pack face upwards in 13 piles of four cards each. Move the Kings to the bottom of their piles, and topple the piles forward so that all four cards may be seen (*see* Fig. 2).

The object of the game is to play the Aces, as they become available, to the centre as foundations and to build ascending suit sequences to the Kings on them.

Only the top card of a pile may be lifted and built on a foundation, or packed in descending sequence, regardless of suit and colour, on the top card of another pile. When all the cards of a pile have been moved, the vacancy is not filled.

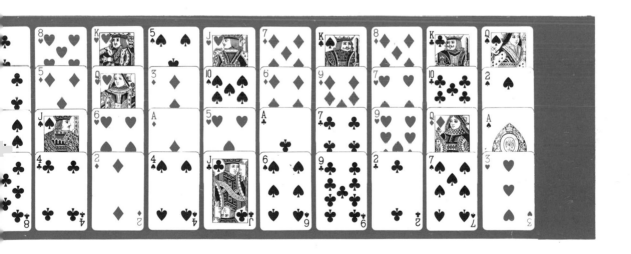

Beleaguered Castle

Beleaguered Castle, also known as Laying Siege and Sham Battle, is an interesting patience with a vertical lay-out.

The four Aces are removed from the pack and placed on the board one above the other to serve as foundations. The

11

remaining 48 cards are dealt face upwards, six cards (which may overlap for convenience) on each side of the Aces (*see* Fig. 3).

The object of the game is to build ascending suit sequences on the Aces to the Kings.

The extreme left-hand and right-hand cards of the rows are exposed. They may be built on the foundations, packed on other exposed cards or be themselves packed on, in descending sequences regardless of suit and colour. Only one card may be moved at a time, and a vacancy caused by all the cards of a row being played may be filled with any exposed card.

Fig. 3 Beleaguered Castle
The 2 ♠ is built on the A ♠, the 8 ♦ packed on the 9 ♥, the J ♦ on the Q ♦, the 7 ♥ on the 8 ♦, the 10 ♦ on the J ♦, the 9 ♦ on the 10 ♦ and the 2 ♥ built on the A ♥.
The 4 ♥ is packed on the 5 ♥. And so on.

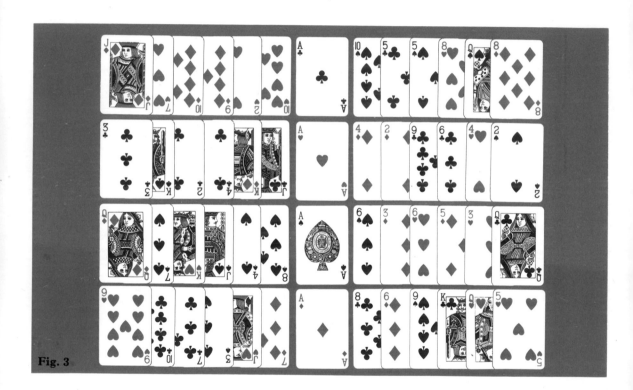

Fig. 3

Belvedere

Remove any Ace from the pack and play it to the centre as the first foundation-card. Deal face upwards to the board 24 cards in eight fans of three cards each (if a King occurs, move it to the bottom of its fan) and three cards in a row, below the lay-out, as a reserve (*see* Fig. 4).

The object of the game is to release the other three Aces, play them to the centre as foundation-cards, and build on the four Aces ascending sequences, regardless of suit and colour, to the Kings.

The top cards of the fans and the cards in the reserve are

12

exposed and may be built on the foundations. In the lay-out, the top cards of the fans may be packed on each other in descending sequences regardless of suit and colour. Only one card may be moved at a time.

A vacancy in the lay-out, when all the cards of a fan have

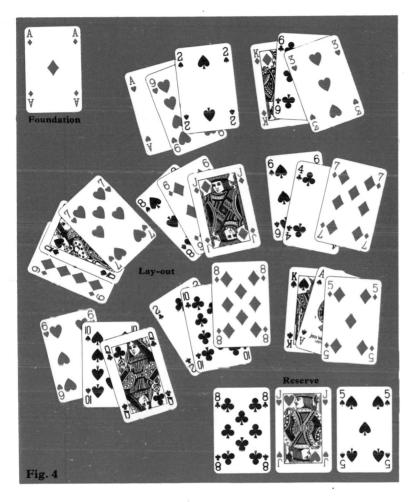

Fig. 4

Fig. 4 Belvedere
The J ♦ is packed on the Q ♣, the 7 ♦ on the 8 ♦, the 6 ♦ on the 7 ♦ and the 5 ♦ on the 6 ♦. The A ♠ is played to the foundation-row and the 2 ♠ built on it.
The 7 ♥ is packed on the 8 ♠, the J ♦ on the Q ♠, the Q ♣ on the K ♠, the J ♦ on the Q ♣, the 10 ♠ on the J ♦ and the 9 ♥ on the 10 ♠.
The A ♥ is played to the foundation-row.
And so on.

been played, is not filled.

The stock is dealt three cards at a time, one card to cover each card of the reserve and to fill any vacancies in it.

The game ends when all the cards in the stock have been dealt.

Bisley

Bisley is generally considered one of the better patiences. The player has an expectation of winning twice in three games.

The pack is dealt face upwards to the board in four rows of 13 cards each, the four Aces, as they occur, being placed at the extreme left of the top row (*see* Fig. 5). As they become

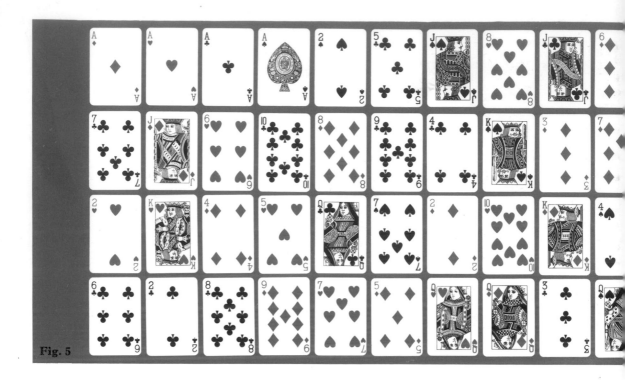

Fig. 5 Bisley
The 2 ♣ may be built on the A ♣ exposing the K ♥, which is played to the centre above the A ♥.
The 3 ♣ is built on the 2 ♣ exposing the K ♦, which is played to the centre above the A ♦.
The Q ♥ is built on the K ♥ exposing the 2 ♦, which is built on the A ♦.
The Q ♦ is built on the K ♦ which exposes the 10 ♥, which is packed on the J ♥.
And so on.

available, the four Kings are placed in a row immediately above their respective Aces.

The object of the game is to build ascending suit sequences on the Aces to Kings and descending suit sequences on the Kings to Aces. It is immaterial where the two sequences meet.

The exposed cards in the bottom row may be built on the foundation-cards, packed on other exposed cards in the lay-out, or be themselves packed on. Packing may be either in ascending or descending suit sequence, which the player may change at his convenience. A vacancy in the lay-out is not filled.

Careful consideration should be given to the lay-out before packing cards because, although every move exposes the card above it, a card that has been packed on blocks the column and a column is not easily unblocked because vacancies in the lay-out are not filled. If no Kings are exposed in the deal, the player's first aim should be to free one. In general, it is best to pack upwards from an 8 and downwards from a 7.

14

Blind

Blind, or Mystery, is a building-up patience with the unusual feature that, before beginning play, the pack is cut and the top card of the cut placed face downwards on the board without its face being seen by the player.

Seven cards are dealt face upwards in a row as the lay-out, and the Aces, as they occur, are played to the centre as foundation-cards (*see* Fig. 6).

The object of the game is to build ascending suit sequences on the Aces to the Kings.

The stock is dealt one card at a time, and any card that cannot be built on a foundation is played to cover one of the cards in the lay-out, at the discretion of the player. Only the top cards of the piles in the lay-out are available to be built on the foundations, but before making a play the cards in the piles may be inspected.

When a vacancy occurs by reason of all the cards of a pile having been played, it is filled either by the next card from the stock or the exposed card from one of the other piles.

Fig. 6

Fig. 6 Blind
The first card of the stock is dealt, and must be played on one of the cards in the lay-out. If possible one should avoid playing a high card on a lower card of the same suit; ideally the cards in the lay-out should be packed in descending suit sequences.

Only one deal is allowed, but when the stock is exhausted and no further builds on the foundations can be made from the lay-out, the face-downwards card (known as the blind) is turned face upwards and is available to be played.

The game offers scope for judgement, because, as far as it is possible to do so, a higher card of a suit should not be played on a pile that contains a lower card of the same suit.

Fig. 7 Block Eleven
Four piles have so far been
blocked by picture cards. Play
continued by placing cards from
the stock on one of the 8s and the
3 ♦, and on the 9 ♠ and 2 ♦.
And so on.

Block Eleven

Block Eleven, or Calling Out, will occupy a couple of minutes of time if you are that unlucky as to have a couple of minutes with nothing better to occupy them.

Remove the first 12 numeral cards from the pack and play them face upwards to the board in three rows of four each, or four rows of three each. Either is as good as the other. Shuffle the rest of the cards until a picture is at the bottom of the pack. Unless the bottom card is a picture the game cannot be won.

Where, added together, two cards in the lay-out total 11, a card is dealt on each from the stock. When a picture card is dealt on one of the piles, no more cards can be dealt on it (*see* Fig. 7). The game is won if all 40 cards of the stock are dealt and the 12 picture cards cover the lay-out.

An inane game with a pretty ending.

Fig. 7

Bridge Patience

In the November, 1927 number of *Auction Bridge Magazine* (now *Bridge Magazine*) C. E. Price mentions that he invented this game 'a year or so ago'. It is a very simple game, that succeeds more often than not, but it is well-spoken of by bridge players because it is an excellent exercise for the memory.

The 52 cards in the pack are dealt into four hands of 13 cards each, as in bridge and whist, and other games of these families. The hands in the North and South quarters of the board are sorted into suits and laid face upwards; those in the West and East quarters are stacked face downwards in two heaps without their faces being looked at (*see* Fig. 8).

The game is played without a trump suit. The West hand leads to the first trick; thereafter the hand that wins a trick leads to the next.

If it can, a hand must follow suit to the card led, and the trick is won by the hand that plays the highest card (Ace high) of the suit that has been led.

The cards in the West and East hands are played from top to bottom of the heaps. When, therefore, the lead is made either by the North or South hand, it will be only by chance if the hands of West and East follow suit.

16

Fig. 8 Bridge Patience

The object of the game is for North and South to win all 13 tricks (the grand slam).

Success depends very largely on remembering the cards played from the hands of West and East, and finessing whenever it is possible to do so. (A finesse may be defined as an attempt to win a trick by playing a card that is not the best of the suit held nor in sequence with it.)

17

The play (the card in bold wins the trick):

W	N	E	S
8♦	**9♦**	K♠	3♦
8♠	**9♣**	J♥	4♣
A♦	**K♣**	9♥	7♣
2♥	**10♣**	4♥	J♣
7♠	2♦	3♣	**Q♣**
5♦	**Q♥**	6♣	5♥
4♦	3♥	7♥	**K♥**
10♥	10♠	8♣	**K♦**
A♣	**8♥**	10♠	6♥
J♦	**A♥**	2♣	2♠
5♣	**Q♦**	6♦	9♠
3♠	**A♠**	7♦	6♠
4♠	5♠	J♠	**Q♠**

The game has been won; mayhap it was too easy.

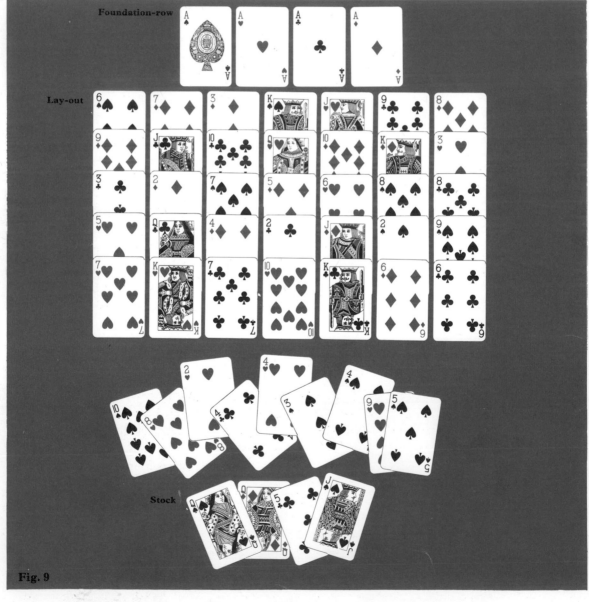

Fig. 9

Brigade

Deal face upwards to the board 35 cards in five rows of seven cards each. Aces, as they are dealt, are played to the centre as a foundation-row. The stock (13 cards in all) may either be placed face upwards on the board, below the lay-out, or held in hand (*see* Fig. 9).

The object of the game is to build on the foundation-cards suit sequences ascending to the Kings.

The exposed cards of the columns may be packed in descending sequences regardless of suit and colour, and may themselves be built on the foundation-cards or packed on exposed cards in the lay-out, so long as they conform to the rules of the game. Cards in the stock may be built on the foundation-cards or packed on the exposed cards in the lay-out. When all the cards of a column have been played, the vacancy must be filled with an exposed card before any further play is made. Only one card may be moved at a time. One waive is permitted: the card lifted is taken into the stock.

Fig. 9 Brigade
The Q ♠ and Q ♦ from the stock may be packed on the K ♥ and K ♣ in the lay-out.
The J ♠ from the stock may be packed either on the Q ♠ or Q ♦ (and preferably on the Q ♦, so not to bury the 2 ♦ in the second column), and the 10 ♥ on the J ♠.
This exposes the 2 ♣ which may be built on its foundation-card.
The 6 ♦ may be packed either on the 7 ♥ or 7 ♣, and the 2 ♠, now exposed, may be built on its foundation-card.
And so on.

Calculation

Calculation—sometimes called Broken Intervals—is well named, because it is necessary to calculate at the turn of every card, and it is a game that calls for more skill than any other patience.

Any Ace, 2, 3 and 4 are removed from the pack and placed on the board in a row. They serve as foundation-cards (*see* Fig. 10).

The object of the game is to build, regardless of suit, the 48 cards of the stock on the Ace in the order: A.2.3.4.5.6.7.8.9.10.J.Q.K.; on the 2 in the order: 2.4.6.8.10.Q.A.3.5.7.9.J.K.; on the 3 in the order: 3.6.9.Q.2.5.8.J.A.4.7.10.K.; and on the 4 in the order: 4.8.Q.3.7.J.2.6.10.A.5.9.K.

The cards in the stock are dealt face upwards one at a time, and any card that cannot be played to a foundation is played to one of four waste-heaps immediately below the foundation-cards. At any time a card may be played from a waste-heap to a foundation, but only the top card of a waste-heap may be played and it must be played to a foundation; it must not be played to another waste-heap. The stock is dealt only once, but when it is exhausted play may continue from the waste-heaps.

If careful consideration is given to the play considerable

progress may be made, because by playing one card from a waste-heap others will become available.

At first it is best to reserve one waste-heap for Kings, because if a King is played on lower cards they are blocked until one of the foundations has been completed. Later in the game, however, the risk of blocking a waste-heap must be taken, because other cards that cannot be played to a foundation have to be accommodated somewhere.

As far as it is possible to do so, the waste-heaps should be

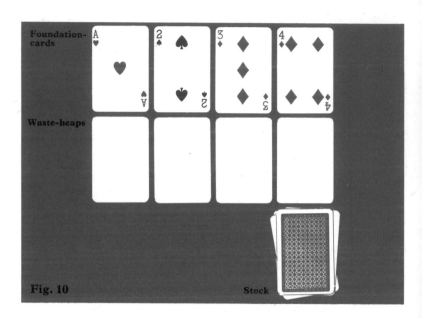

Fig. 10 Calculation

packed with descending sequences. Of course they cannot extend very far, but even a descending sequence of four or five cards will usually prove helpful.

It is important to keep in mind how soon or how late a card will be needed. If, for example, the first card from the stock is a 10 it should go to the waste-heap under the 2 of Spades, because it will be needed to be built on this foundation sooner than it will on the other three.

Unless it is necessary to maintain a sequence, one should avoid playing a card to a waste-heap that already contains a card of the same rank.

The Carpet

Remove the four Aces from the pack and play them to the centre as foundations. Below them deal face upwards 20 cards in four rows of five cards each (*see* Fig. 11).

The object of the game is to build ascending suit sequences on the Aces to the Kings.

20

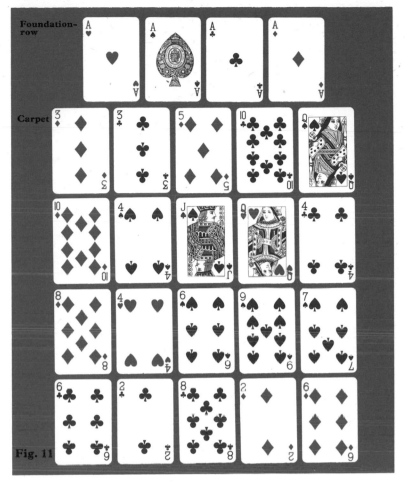

Fig. 11 The Carpet
The 2 ♣ is built on the A ♣, the 3 ♣ on the 2 ♣ and the 4 ♣ on the 3 ♣.
The 2 ♦ is built on the A ♦ and the 3 ♦ on the 2 ♦.
And so on.

All the cards in the lay-out (the carpet) are available to be built on the foundations, and the vacancies filled from the waste-heap, or from the stock if there is no waste-heap.

There is no packing on the lay-out. The stock is turned one card at a time and any card that cannot be built on a foundation is played to a waste-heap, the top card of which is always available to be played.

The game ends when the stock has been dealt once.

Crossword

The 12 court cards are removed from the pack and temporarily set aside. The top card of the pack is played to the board, and the rest of the pack is turned one card at a time. Each card in turn is played to the board in a position that touches a card already played, either at top or bottom, either side, or at a corner.

The object of the game is to complete a square—seven

21

Fig. 12

Fig. 12 Crossword

cards each way—in which the pips of the cards, in each row and column, add up to an even number. The court cards do not count. They are brought into the game when needed to serve as stops, in the same way as the black squares in a crossword puzzle; at least nine, and probably all of them, will have to be used. The pips of the cards between two court cards, or between a court card and the outer edge of the square, must also add up to an even number (*see* Fig. 12).

When 48 cards have been played there will be four cards left in hand and only one square to fill. The player may look at the cards and choose which one of them he needs to complete the game.

An ill-favour'd thing, sir, but mine own.

22

Demon

Demon is one of the best known of the single-pack patience games. It is sometimes called Fascination and sometimes Thirteen. In the U.S.A. it is known as Canfield because it was reputedly invented by Richard A. Canfield, a gambler of the late nineteenth century, whose practice it was to sell the pack for $52.00 and pay $5.00 for every card in the foundation-row when the game ended. It was far from the profitable business that it appears on the surface because he had to employ a large number of croupiers to keep an eye on every player.

Thirteen cards are dealt face downwards on the board in a

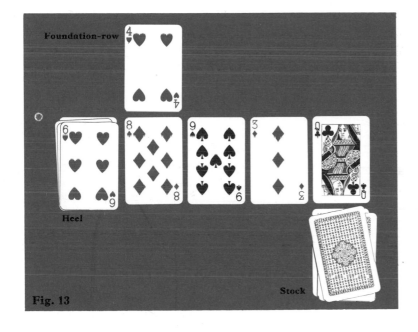

Fig. 13

Fig. 13 Demon
The 8 ♦ is packed on the 9 ♠, and the vacancy filled by the 6 ♥. The card under the 6 ♥ is faced and becomes available for play.

pile, and the top card is turned face upwards. This is the heel. To the right of it, four cards are dealt face upwards in a row. The next card of the pack is dealt face upwards and placed immediately above the first card of the row. It determines the foundation-cards, and the other three cards of the same rank, as they become available, are placed in line with it (see Fig. 13).

The object of the game is to build ascending, round-the-corner suit sequences on the foundation-cards. The four cards to the right of the heel are packed in descending, round-the-corner sequences of alternate colour. The bottom card of a column is exposed. It may be built on a foundation, packed on the bottom card of another column, or itself be packed on. A sequence may be moved from one column to another only as a whole, and only if it can be packed on the next higher card of a different colour.

The top card of the heel is exposed and available for building on a foundation or packing on a column. When all the cards of a column have been moved, the vacancy must be filled immediately with the top card of the heel, and the card under it faced and made available for play. When the heel is exhausted, a vacancy is filled with the top card of the waste-heap and the player is no longer under the obligation of filling the vacancy immediately.

The cards in the stock are turned face upwards in batches of three to a waste-heap, the top card of which is always available for play. If there is less than three cards at the end of the stock they are turned singly. The stock is dealt and redealt until the game succeeds or is lost because no further move can be made. One grace, however, is allowed. A player may take one card from the top of a foundation-pile and place it either at the top or bottom of one of the columns, so long as it is in sequence with the card next to it and of the opposite colour.

Demon is not an easy game. The player has only about one chance in 30 of succeeding. The chance of success, however, may be improved by:
1. Dealing the 13 cards to the heel face upwards in a column.
2. Packing a part-sequence from one column onto another.
3. Not being under an obligation to fill a vacancy from the heel immediately.

Racing Demon
In the U.S.A. Racing Demon is known as Pounce. It is not so much a game of patience but a party game for any reasonable number of players.

Each has a pack of cards, which, for convenience of sorting, should be of different design or colour. The players play a game of demon patience simultaneously, but with the Aces as foundation-cards and as common property on which any player may build. The winner is he who is first to dispose of the cards in his heel. (It is advisable to draw up a strict code of rules before play begins. Long finger nails can do a lot of damage; assault and battery is to be discouraged!) Quickness of the eye and speed of the hand count for much.

Divorce

Deal one card at a time face upwards to any one of four waste-heaps. As they occur the Aces and 2s are played to the centre as foundation-cards, placing the 2s alongside the Aces of the same suit.

The object of the game is to build ascending sequences of alternate colour and rank on each of the foundation-cards. In this way a red Ace is built up to a red King by way of a black 3, a red 5, a black 7, a red 9 and a black Knave; and a black Ace to a black King by way of a red 3, a black 5, a red 7, a black 9 and a red Knave. Similarly, a black 2 is built up to a red Queen by way of a red 4, a black 6, a red 8 and a black 10; and a red 2 to a black Queen by way of a black 4, a red 6, a black 8 and a red 10 (see Fig. 14).

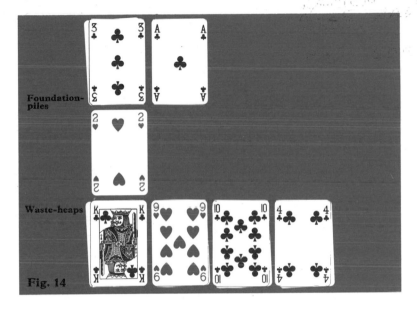

Fig. 14 **Divorce**
Three foundation-cards have been played to the centre, and the 3 ♣ built on the A ♥.
The 4 ♣ is built on the 2 ♥, exposing the 5 ♠.
The next card from the stock (2 ♦) is placed above the 10 ♣.
And so on.

If the Aces and 2s have been placed alongside each other, the game, if successful, will end with the two red Queens by the side of the two black Kings, and the two black Queens by the side of the two red Kings. Quite topical!

Eagle Wings

Eagle Wings, or Thirteen Down, is one of those games that depends for success entirely on the fortuitous order of the cards.

Thirteen cards are dealt to the board face downwards in a pile (the heel). On each side of the heel four cards are dealt face upwards in a row (the wings). Above the heel a card is dealt face upwards as the first foundation (see Fig. 15). As they become available the other three cards of the same rank will be placed in the row with it.

25

The object of the game is to build on the foundation-cards complete suits in round-the-corner sequences. The eight cards in the wings are available to be played to the foundations, and the vacancies are filled with cards from the heel turned face upwards. The stock is dealt one card at a time, and any card that cannot be played to a foundation is played to a waste-heap. When only one card remains in the heel it is turned face upwards and may be played direct to a foundation and without first filling a vacancy in the wings. When the heel is exhausted a vacancy in the wings may be

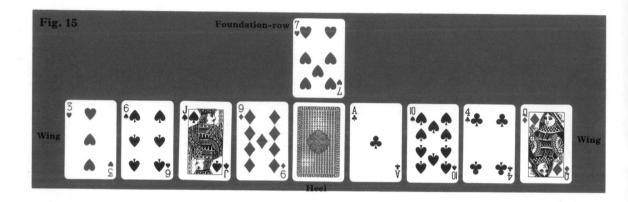

Fig. 15 Eagle Wings

filled either with a card from the stock or from the waste-heap.

The stock may be dealt three times in all, but must not be shuffled between deals.

You won't win!

Easy Go

Play the four Aces to the centre as foundation-cards. Below them deal face upwards to the board 12 cards in any arrangement that is convenient (*see* Fig. 16).

The object of the game is to build ascending suit sequences on the Aces to the Kings.

All the cards in the lay-out are exposed and may be built on the foundations. They may also be packed on each other in descending suit sequences, but only one card at a time may be moved from one pile in the lay-out to another. A vacancy in the lay-out is filled either from the waste-heap or the stock.

The stock is dealt one card at a time, and a card that cannot be built on a foundation nor packed on the lay-out is played to a waste-heap, the top card of which is always available to be played.

26

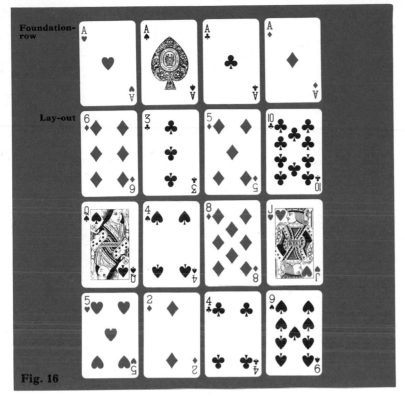

Fig. 16

Fig. 16 Easy Go
The 2 ♦ is built on the A ♦.
The 3 ♣ is packed on the 4 ♣ and
the 5 ♦ on the 6 ♦.
If the 7 ♦ is dealt from the stock
it may be packed on the 8 ♦, but
the 6 ♦ with the 5 ♦ cannot be
packed on the 7 ♦.
And so on.

Eight Off

A fascinating game for an idle quarter of an hour, with an estimated chance of winning one out of every two games.

Deal the pack face upwards to the board in six overlapping rows of eight cards each, playing the Aces as they occur to a foundation-row (see Fig. 17).

The object of the game is to build suit sequences on the Aces to the Kings.

The bottom card of a column is exposed and, after it has been played, the card immediately above it is exposed and available. It is a feature of the game that the player may take into his hand any number of exposed cards up to eight—but not more than eight. These cards are collectively known as the reserve; they are retained in hand until such time as they are required for building on a foundation or for packing on an exposed card in a column.

An exposed card at the foot of a column may be built on a foundation, packed on another exposed card or itself be packed on, in descending suit sequence. Only one card may be moved at a time.

A vacancy, caused by all the cards of a column being played, is filled by a King.

27

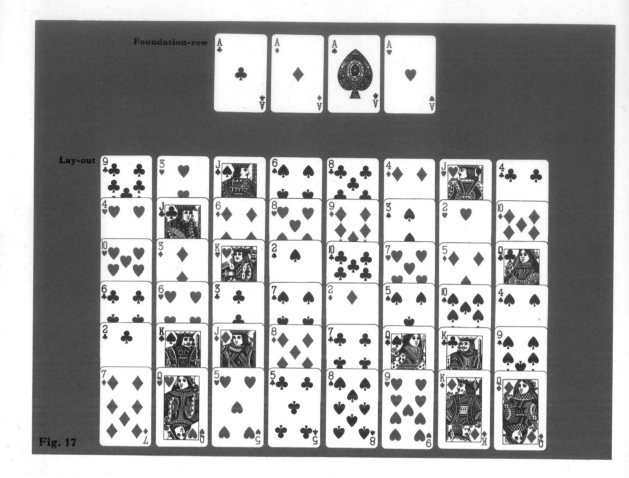

Fig. 17

Fig. 17 Eight Off

The Q ♦ is packed on the K ♦, the 8 ♠ on the 9 ♠ and the 5 ♣ taken into the reserve.

The 7 ♦ is packed on the 8 ♦ and the 2 ♣ built on the A ♣.

The 5 ♥ is taken into the reserve, the J ♦ packed on the Q ♦ and the 3 ♣ built on the 2 ♣.

The 7 ♦ and 8 ♦ are taken into the reserve, the 7 ♠ packed on the 8 ♠ and the 2 ♠ built on the A ♠. And so on.

A player's first aim should be to release low cards and build them on the foundations. Retain as many openings as possible in the reserve – they are more important than vacancies in the lay-out that may be filled only by a King.

Florentine

Deal five cards face upwards to the board in the form of a cross. The sixth card is dealt to the centre and denotes the foundations (*see* Fig. 18).

The object of the game is to build ascending, round-the-corner suit sequences on the foundation-cards.

The card in the centre of the cross may not be packed on, but the other four cards of the cross may in descending sequence regardless of suit and colour. When one of these cards is built on a foundation, or packed on another card of the cross, the vacancy is filled either with the top card of

28

Foundation-cards

Fig. 18

Waste-heap

Fig. 18 Florentine
The foundation-cards are built up
to their respective 7s.
The 6 ♦ is packed on the 7 ♠ and
the vacancy filled with the 10 ♠,
or with the 2 ♣ and the 10 ♠
played to the centre of the cross.
And so on.

the waste-heap or with the centre card of the cross and the
vacancy in the centre of the cross filled with the top card of
the waste-heap.

One redeal is allowed, but no shuffling.

The Flower Garden

The Flower Garden, sometimes called the Bouquet or
Garden, is generally recognized as one of the better
patiences, and offers the player a chance of success in every
two games.

Deal face upwards to the board six fans of six cards each.
The stock of 16 cards is held in hand (*see* Fig. 19). For
convenience, the fans on the board are known as the beds,
and the stock in hand as the bouquet. All the cards in the
bouquet and on the extreme right of the beds are exposed.

The object of the game is to release the Aces and play them

29

Fig. 19

Beds

Bouquet

Fig. 19 The Flower Garden

Play the A ♥ to the foundation-row.

Pack the 5 ♦ on the 6 ♣ and play the A ♣ to the foundation-row.

Pack the Q ♠ on the K ♦, the J ♥ on the Q ♠ and play the A ♠ to the foundation-row.

Pack the 6 ♣ with the 5 ♦ on the 7 ♣ and build the 2 ♠ on the A ♠.

to the centre as foundations, to be built on in ascending suit sequences to the Kings.

The exposed cards of the beds are packed in descending sequences regardless of suit. A sequence may be moved from one bed to another only as a whole and provided the sequential order is retained. When all the cards of a bed have been played, the vacancy may be filled by any available card or sequence.

30

As far as it is possible to do so, cards from the bouquet should not be packed on the beds, because it decreases the number of cards that are available at any one time: they should be reserved for building on the foundations. For the same reason, it is not always wise to pack many cards on the beds in order to make a vacancy to begin another bed: it may prove very costly. The early moves should be directed towards releasing the Aces and other low cards, because even a single low card under a high one may block the game.

Fortune

Remove the four Aces from the pack and play them to the centre as foundation-cards. Below them deal face upwards

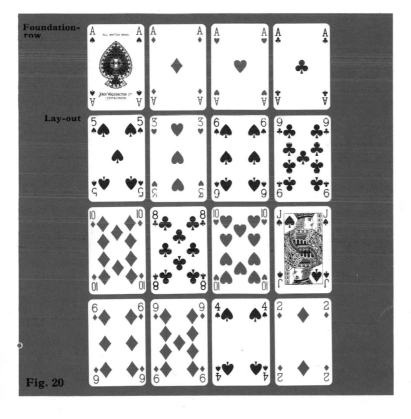

Fig. 20 Fortune
The 2 ◆ is built on the A ◆.
The 5 ♠ is packed on the 6 ♠ and the 4 ♠ on the 5 ♠.
The 8 ♣ is packed on the 9 ♣, and the 9 ◆ on the 10 ◆.
And so on.

12 cards, which, for convenience, may be arranged on the board in three rows of four cards each (*see* Fig. 20).

The object of the game is to build ascending suit sequences on the Aces to the Kings.

The cards in the lay-out are available to be built on the foundations, or packed in descending suit sequences. Only one card may be moved at a time.

The stock is dealt one card at a time and any that cannot be

31

built on a foundation nor packed on the lay-out is played to a waste-heap, the top card of which is always available for play.

A vacancy in the lay-out is filled with the top card of the waste-heap, or a card from the stock if there is no waste-heap.

Only one deal is allowed.

Golf Patience

Deal face upwards to the board 35 cards in five rows of seven cards each, that may overlap for convenience. They form the

Fig. 21 Golf Patience
Pack the 8 ♣ on the 9 ♥, the 7 ♥ on the 8 ♣, the 8 ♠ on the 7 ♥ and the 9 ♣ on the 8 ♠.
As no further move is possible, the next card of the stock is dealt to the waste-heap.
And so on.

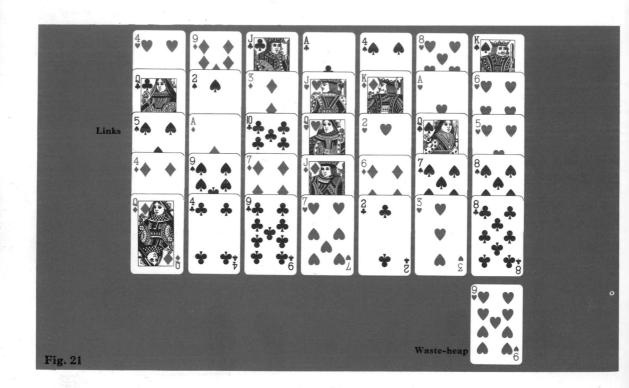

Links

Waste-heap

Fig. 21

links. The first card of the stock is dealt face upwards to the board to begin the waste-heap (*see* Fig. 21).

The object of the game is to remove all the cards from the links by packing on the exposed card of the waste-heap the exposed cards in the links. The cards may be packed in ascending or descending sequences, irrespective of suit, and the option of direction extends at every play; round-the-corner sequences, however, are disallowed.

When no further packing on the waste-heap is possible,

Fig. 22 Grandfather's Clock
The Q ♠ may be built on the J ♠, the A ♣ on the K ♣, the 4 ♠ on the 3 ♠, the 7 ♥ on the 6 ♥, the 9 ♦ on the 8 ♦, the 10 ♦ on the 9 ♦ and the K ♠ on the Q ♠.
The Q ♥ may be packed on the K ♥, the K ♦ built on the Q ♦, the 2 ♠ may be packed on the 3 ♣ and the J ♦ built on the 10 ♦.
And so on.

32

Foundation-cards

Lay-out

Fig. 22

33

the next card of the stock is dealt to it and packed. The game is won if the player clears all the cards from the links.

Competitive Golf Patience

Like golf itself, golf patience is a much better game when played competitively.

Before play begins the players must decide whether they will play a match of 9 holes or 18 holes, and whether they will determine the result by what golfers call match play or medal play.

Each player has a pack of cards and plays simultaneously. When all 17 cards of the stock have been dealt and packed, the number of cards left in the links is the player's score for the hole. The pack is shuffled and redealt for the next hole.

If, as sometimes happens, the links is cleared before the player has dealt all the cards in the stock to the waste-heap, the number of cards left in the stock counts in the player's favour and, at the end of the match, is deducted from the total score for his round.

Although the game is usually played only by two players, with a little ingenuity three-ball matches and foursomes may be arranged.

Grandfather's Clock

Remove from the pack the 2, 6 and 10 of Hearts, the 3, 7 and Knave of Spades, the 4, 8 and Queen of Diamonds and the 5, 9 and King of Clubs; arrange them on the board face upwards in a circle comparable to the hours on the face of a clock, with the 9 of Clubs at noon, and the others in sequence round the dial. They serve as foundation-cards to be built on in ascending, round-the-corner suit sequences until each reaches the number appropriate to its position on the dial, the Knave representing 11 o'clock and the Queen noon. (The 10, Knave, Queen and King foundations will each need four cards built on them, the others only three cards.) The remaining 40 cards are dealt face upwards below them, in eight rows of five cards each, that for convenience may overlap (*see* Fig. 22).

The cards at the bottom of each column are available to be built on a foundation, be packed on, or themselves packed on other exposed cards, in descending, round-the-corner sequences regardless of suit. Only one card may be moved at a time. If all the cards of one column have been moved, the vacancy may be filled by any available card.

King Albert

King Albert has been given the alternative name of Idiot's Delight. Why is hard to know because Basil Dalton, an Oxford don who wrote a number of books on patience and other card games, describes it as one of the less mechanical and more intelligent games of patience. Writing in 1948 he expressed the opinion that it was quite the best single-pack game yet invented.

The game is similar to Raglan (*see* p. 52) but is rather more difficult.

Forty-five cards are dealt to the board face upwards in rows of nine cards, eight cards, seven cards, and so down to a single card. For convenience the cards may overlap. The remaining seven cards, known as the reserve, may either

(see p. 52)

Fig. 23 King Albert

The 6 ♠ is packed on the 7 ♦, the J ♣ on the Q ♥ and the A ♥ played to the foundation-row. The 10 ♥ is packed on the J ♣ and the A ♠ played to the foundation-row.
The 9 ♠ is packed on the 10 ♥, the 8 ♥ on the 9 ♠, the 7 ♠ on the 8 ♥, the 6 ♦ on the 7 ♠ and the 5 ♠ on the 6 ♦.
The vacancy is filled with the K ♠, the 4 ♦, from the reserve, is packed on the 5 ♠, the 3 ♣ on the 4 ♦ and the A ♣ played to the foundation-row.
And so on.

Lay-out

Reserve

Fig. 23

be held in hand or placed face upwards on the board in front of the player (*see* Fig. 23).

The object of the game is to release the Aces, play them to the centre as foundations, and build on them ascending suit sequences to the Kings.

The cards at the bottom of the columns are exposed. They may be built on the foundations, packed on other exposed cards or be themselves packed on, in descending sequences of alternate colour. Only one card may be moved at a time. A vacancy caused by moving all the cards of a column may be filled by any available card. The cards in the reserve are available for building on a foundation or packing on the exposed cards in the lay-out.

Klondike

Klondike is one of the best-known one-pack patience games. It is sometimes called Triangle, which is understandable from the lay-out, and sometimes The Chinaman, which is not.

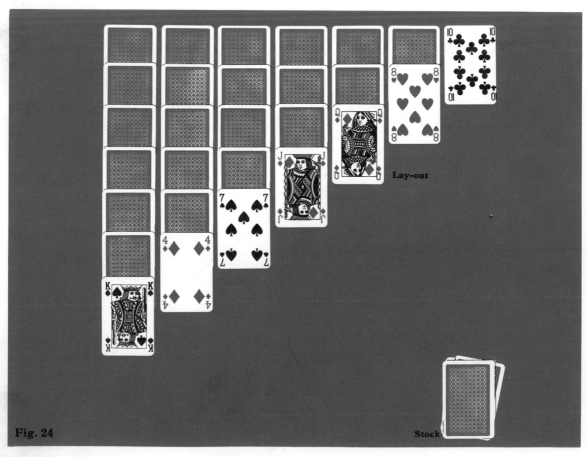

Fig. 24

Lay-out

Stock

Twenty-eight cards are dealt face downwards to the board in seven overlapping rows, the first row of seven cards, the second of six cards, and so down to a single card in the last row. The bottom card of each column is then turned face upwards (*see* Fig. 24).

As the Aces become available they are played to the centre as foundations, the object of the game being to build them up in suit sequences to the Kings.

The faced cards at the bottom of the columns are available to be built on the foundations, packed on other faced cards, or themselves be packed on, in descending sequences of alternate colour. A sequence may be moved only as a whole. When a faced card or a sequence is moved from the bottom of a column, the card under it is turned face upwards and becomes available for play. A vacancy caused by moving all the cards from a column may be filled only by a King or a sequence headed by a King.

The stock is turned one card at a time to a waste-heap, the top card of which is available for play. Only one deal is allowed.

Aces must be played to the foundation-row when they become available. Other cards need not be played at once: they may be left in position in the prospect of finding a better move for them later in the game.

As the game is rather a difficult one, with a chance of success of only once in about 30 games, it may be made easier by moving sequences in part, and dealing the stock three times.

Fig. 24 Klondike
The 7 ♠ is packed on the 8 ♥ and the card under the 7 ♠ faced. The 10 ♣ is packed on the J ♦, the vacancy filled by the K ♠ and the card under the K ♠ faced. The Q ♦ is packed on the K ♠ and the card under the Q ♦ faced. And so on.

Joker Klondike

Joker Klondike is one of the best of the several variations of Klondike. It is played in the same way as the parent game but with the Joker included in the pack. Whenever the Joker becomes available it must be played to a foundation (it may be played to whichever foundation the player thinks best) and the cards in correct sequence are built on it. When the natural card becomes available it replaces the Joker, which is built on another foundation.

If the Joker becomes available before an Ace has been played to the foundation-row, it must remain in position until an Ace is available and a foundation started.

La Belle Lucie

La Belle Lucie, but I have no idea who Lucy was, is one of the classical single-pack patiences. (It is given first place in Lady Adelaide Cadogan's *Illustrated Games of Patience* (circa

Fig. 25

Fig. 25 *La Belle Lucie*

The 9 ♠ is packed on the 10 ♠,
the 8 ♠ on the 9 ♠ and the A ♥
is played to the foundation-row.
The 7 ♣ is packed on the 8 ♣, the
6 ♣ on the 7 ♣ and the 5 ♣ on the
6 ♣.
The 2 ♥ is built on the A ♥, the
4 ♣ is packed on the 5 ♣ and the
A ♣ played to the foundation-row.
The 10 ♦ is packed on the J ♦
and the 2 ♣ built on the A ♣.
And so on.

1870).) Known also as the Fan, Clover Leaf, Alexander the Great and Midnight Oil, its popularity is unquestioned.

Deal the whole pack face upwards to the board in 17 fans of three cards each, and a single card (*see* Fig. 25). The extreme right-hand cards of the fans and the single card are exposed.

The object of the game is to release the Aces, play them to the centre as foundations, and build on them ascending suit sequences to the Kings.

An exposed card in the lay-out may be built on a foundation, packed in descending suit sequence on another exposed card, or itself be packed on in descending suit sequence. A vacancy made by playing all the cards of a fan is not filled.

When all possible moves have been made the cards in the lay-out—but not those in the foundation-row—are picked up, shuffled and redealt in fans of three cards each. If one or two cards are in excess, they make a separate fan. Altogether three deals are allowed, and after the last a player has the grace of drawing a buried card out of a fan.

Play calls for care because there is the risk that when playing to release one card a more important one may be buried deeply. Before making a move the lay-out should be examined and play directed towards releasing the most cards possible.

Labyrinth

Labyrinth is quite a simple game and nothing like as tortuous as its name suggests.

The four Aces are played to the centre as foundation-cards, to be built on in ascending suit sequences to the Kings. Below them eight cards are dealt to the board face upwards in a row. Available cards are built on the foundations and the vacancies filled from the stock.

When available cards (if any) have been built on the foundations and vacancies filled, a second row of eight cards is dealt below the first. Cards from it are built on the foundations, but vacancies are not filled; it is only vacancies in the first row that are filled.

Dealing and building on the foundations is continued in this way until the stock is exhausted.

The cards in the top and bottom rows are exposed and built on the foundations, and when a card is played from the top row it exposes the card below it, and when from the bottom row the card above it. As only vacancies in the first row are filled, during the game there may be a number of

Fig. 26

unfilled vacancies in the lay-out (*see* Fig. 26). It may suggest a labyrinth.

The game succeeds if all four foundations are built up to the Kings. Only one deal is allowed, and if the game has not been won when the stock has been exhausted, the player has the grace of playing any one card from the lay-out to a foundation.

Little Spider

The two red Aces and the two black Kings (or the black Aces and red Kings) are removed from the pack and placed face upwards in a row on the board, to serve as foundations. The remaining 48 cards are dealt face upwards in two rows of four cards each, one above the foundation-cards, the other below them (*see* Fig. 27).

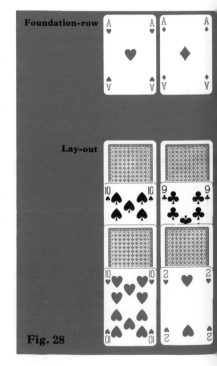

Fig. 28

Fig. 26 Labyrinth

The 3 ♠ is built on the 2 ♠, the 4 ♥ on the 3 ♥ exposing the 4 ♠ which is built on the 3 ♠.
The 5 ♥ is built on the 4 ♥, the 6 ♥ on the 5 ♥, the 7 ♥ on the 6 ♥, and the 8 ♥ on the 7 ♥.
And so on.

Fig. 27 Little Spider

The Q ♠ may be built on the K ♠ and the 2 ♦ on the A ♦.
The 8 ♥ may be packed on the 9 ♣ and the 5 ♦ on the 6 ♥.
And so on.

Fig. 28 Martha

The 2 ♥ is built on the A ♥ and the face-downwards card turned.
The 2 ♣ is built on the A ♣ and the face-downwards card turned.
The 9 ♠ is packed on the 10 ♥, the 8 ♥ on the 9 ♠, the 7 ♣ on the 8 ♥ and the face-downwards cards turned after each move.
And so on.

The object of the game is to build ascending suit sequences on the Aces to the Kings, and descending suit sequences on the Kings to the Aces.

The cards are dealt face upwards. After every batch of eight cards has been dealt, the top cards of the eight piles are available. Those in the upper row may be built on any foundation, but those in the lower row may be built only on

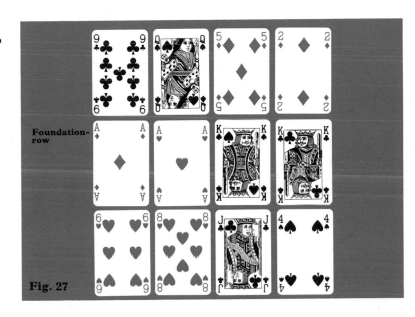

Fig. 27

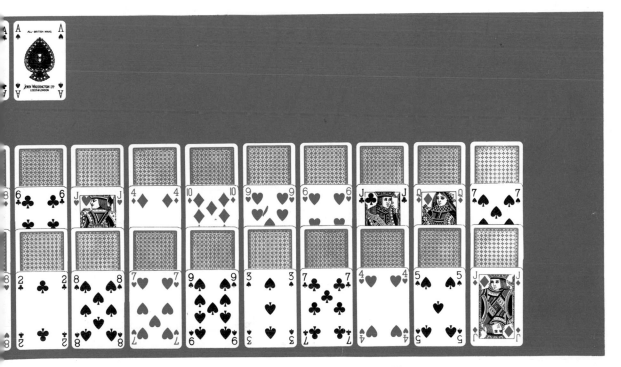

41

the foundation immediately above it. Exposed cards in the lay-out may be packed on any other exposed cards, either in ascending or descending, round-the-corner sequences regardless of suit. A vacancy in the lay-out, made by moving all the cards in a pile, is not filled.

Martha

Remove the Aces from the pack and play them to the centre as foundation-cards. Deal the rest of the pack in 12 columns of four cards each, the first and third cards of each column face downwards, the second and fourth face upwards. The rows may overlap for convenience (see Fig. 28).

The object of the game is to build ascending suit sequences on the Aces to the Kings.

The bottom cards of the columns are available to be built on the foundations, packed on the exposed cards in the lay-out, and themselves be packed on, in descending sequences of alternate colour. Provided the sequential order and alternation of colour are retained a sequence may be moved either wholly or in part from one column to another. A vacancy in the lay-out, however, may be filled only by a single card. The cards in the lay-out that are dealt face downwards are turned face upwards when the cards below them are played.

Maze

Although I am not prepared to agree with those who say that Maze is the best of the single-pack patiences, it is certainly one of them, because, if the player is skilful, he will succeed far more often than not.

The whole pack is dealt face upwards to the board in six rows, the first and second of eight cards each, the third, fourth, fifth and sixth of nine cards each. The four Kings are discarded from the lay-out to leave four vacancies, making six in all because there are vacancies at the extreme right of the first and second rows (see Fig. 29).

By moving one card at a time into a vacancy, the object of the game is to arrange the 48 cards into four ascending suit sequences (each from Ace to Queen) beginning with an Ace

Fig. 29

at the extreme left of the first row to a Queen at the extreme right of the sixth row. The sequence follows on from the end of one row to the row below it, and not only is it assumed that the rows are continuous, as in reading and writing, but that the sixth row is continuous with the first.

Only one card may be moved at a time. It may be taken from anywhere in the lay-out and moved to any vacancy provided it is in suit sequence one higher than the card on the left of the vacancy to which it is being moved, or one lower than the card on the right of the vacancy. When a vacancy occurs on the right of a Queen, it may be filled with an Ace, as an alternative to the card one lower in suit sequence than the card on the right of the vacancy.

Fig. 29 Maze

Vacancy 1 may be filled either with any Ace or the 6 ♦ or the 9 ♥.
Vacancy 2 may be filled either with the 8 ♥ or 2 ♥.
Vacancy 3 may be filled either with the 5 ♥ or 8 ♦.
Vacancy 4 may be filled either with the 5 ♠ or 7 ♦.
Vacancy 5 may be filled either with any Ace or the 4 ♠.
Vacancy 6 may be filled either with the J ♥ or 4 ♥.
Computer programmers will be able to enjoy themselves.

43

Fig. 30(a) Monte Carlo
The 3 ◆ may be discarded with
the 3 ♣, the Q ♠ either with the
Q ♣ or Q ◆ and is better
discarded with the Q ◆ to bring
the 8 ◆ and 8 ♠ together after
consolidation.
The 10 ◆ is discarded with the
10 ♥ and the 4 ♠ with the 4 ◆.

Fig. 30(a)

Monte Carlo

Monte Carlo, Weddings or Double or Quits, is a rather
simple patience that calls for very little skill.

Fig. 30(b)

Fig. 30(b) Monte Carlo
The three vacancies in the third
row and the five in the fourth row
are filled from the stock.
The 2 ◆ is discarded with the
2 ♣, and the 8 ◆ with the 8 ♠.
And so on.

44

Twenty cards are dealt face upwards to the board in four rows of five cards each (*see* Fig. 30(a)).

The object of the game is to discard the whole pack. Any two cards of the same rank that touch each other, either at top or bottom, at either side or at any one of the four corners, are discarded. The lay-out is consolidated by closing up the rows from right to left and from a lower row to the one above it—taking care not to alter the order of the cards—and the vacancies filled with cards from the stock (*see* Fig. 30(b)).

If three cards of the same rank touch each other the player may choose which two he will discard. It is best to discard the pair that will give more additional plays after the lay-out has been consolidated.

The game is won if the whole pack is discarded. It's fun even though the odds are against you, and if no pair touches in the first 20 cards the game is lost before it started.

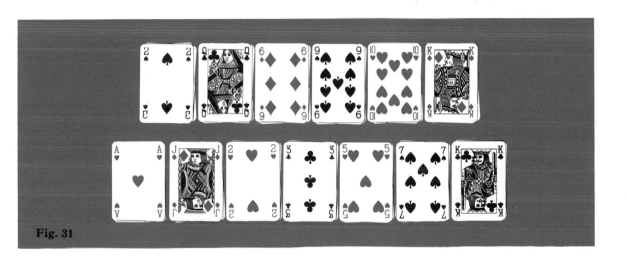

Fig. 31

Ninety-one

The game is not a difficult one, but not to be recommended to anyone who cannot do simple arithmetic without using fingers, nor as a sedative for an accountant after a hard day in the office.

The pack is divided into 13 packets of four cards each, which are laid face upwards on the table (*see* Fig. 31). Counting the King as 13, the Queen as 12, the Knave as 11, and the other cards according to their pips, the object of the game is to move the top cards from packet to packet until you reach a total of exactly 91. A sequence from Ace to King fills the bill, but so will many other combinations.

Fig. 31 Ninety-one
The total is 94, so the player needs to lose 3.
Suppose he lifts the 10 ♥ and the card under it is the 3 ♠.
He has lost 7, making his total 87. He needs to gain 4 so he puts the 10 ♥ on top of the 6 ♦, which makes the total 91.
Q.E.D.

Fig. 32

Lay-out

Waste-heap

One Foundation

Deal face upwards to the board 35 cards in five overlapping rows of seven cards each. The thirty-sixth card is dealt face upwards to begin a waste-heap (*see* Fig. 32).

The cards at the foot of the columns are exposed, and the object of the game is to clear the lay-out of all cards by packing the exposed cards on the waste-heap in ascending or descending sequences irrespective of suit and colour. The direction of a sequence may be reversed at any time, with the exception that an Ace cannot be packed on a King nor a King on an Ace. There is no packing on the exposed cards in the lay-out.

When all available cards in the lay-out have been packed on the waste-heap, another card is dealt from the stock to the waste-heap, and play continues in this way until the stock is exhausted. The game then ends, unless the lay-out has been cleared first.

Fig. 32 One Foundation
The 9 ♥ is packed on the 10 ♦, the 8 ♠ on the 9 ♥, the 7 ♠ on the 8 ♠, the 6 ♥ on the 7 ♠ and the 7 ♣ on the 6 ♥.
And so on.

Out for the Count

Remove the 12 picture cards from the pack.

Deal face upwards to the board a row of three cards. If any Spades occur in the row discard them and fill the vacancies from the stock. When a row has been dealt, and

46

vacancies filled, so that it contains no Spades, deal another row below it in the same way. When six rows have been dealt, the Spades discarded and the vacancies filled, pick up the 18 cards, shuffle them together with the cards left in the stock and redeal. (*See* Fig. 33.)

A second redeal, made in the same way, is allowed, and the game is won if all 10 Spades are discarded.

usque ad nauseam.

Fig. 33 Out for the Count
The third row has just been dealt. The 5 ♠ and 10 ♠ are discarded, and the two vacancies filled from the stock.
And so on.

Fig. 33

Poker Patience

The top card of the pack is placed face upwards anywhere on the board. The next 24 cards are turned face upwards one at a time and each, as it is turned, is placed on the board in any position so long as it touches at top or bottom, either side, or any of the four corners, a card previously played.

The object of the game is to make a square of five cards each way to form poker hands (*see* Fig. 34) in each row and each column.

Two methods of scoring are recognized:

Hands	*Points*	
	English	American
Royal Straight Flush	30	100
Straight Flush	30	75
Four of a Kind (Fours)	16	50
Full House	10	25
Flush	5	20
Straight	12	15
Three of a Kind (Threes)	6	10
Two Pairs	3	5
One Pair	1	2

The English scoring is based on the relative difficulty of forming hands in poker patience, the American on the relative likelihood of the hands in the standard game of poker.

A score of 70 points (English) or 200 (American) may be counted as a win.

Competitive Poker Patience

Poker patience is at its best when played competitively. Indeed, in Edwardian days, when radio and television were unknown and motor cars and the cinematograph were in their infancies, the game had a big vogue. Matches and tournaments were played, and even leagues were formed.

Any number of players may take part. Each has a pack of cards. One player calls the card as he draws it from the pack and the others draw the same card from their packs and

Fig. 34 Poker Patience

Royal Straight Flush The top five cards of any one of the four suits.

Straight Flush Five cards of the same suit in sequence.

Four of a Kind Four cards of the same rank and an odd card.

Full House Three cards of the same rank and two of another.

Flush Any five cards of the same suit.

Straight Five cards in sequence, the suits immaterial.

Three of a Kind Three cards of the same rank and two odd cards.

Two Pairs Two cards of the same rank, two other cards of the same rank and an odd card.

One Pair Two cards of the same rank and three odd cards.

Fig. 34

48

arrange it on the board in front of them. When all 25 cards have been called, the players total their scores and the highest wins.

Puss in the Corner

Remove the four Aces and play them full square in the centre of the board. They serve as foundations to be built on in ascending colour (not necessarily suit) sequences to the Kings. Four cards are dealt to the board to begin waste-heaps, and, by tradition, they are placed at the corners of the foundation-square (*see* Fig. 35).

Four cards are dealt, one at a time, from the stock and played on any of the waste-heaps. The top cards of the waste-heaps are available to be built on the foundations. Continue dealing in this way—building available cards on the foundations after every four have been dealt—until the stock is exhausted.

One redeal is allowed. The waste-heaps may be picked up in any order and redealt without shuffling.

Keep one waste-heap for high cards and, whenever possible, prefer to play a card on a higher rather than on a lower one.

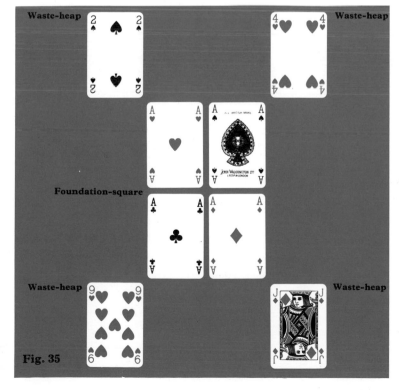

Waste-heap 2♠ 2♠

Waste-heap 4♥ 4♥

A♥ A♥ A♠ A♠

Foundation-square

A♣ A♣ A♦ A♦

Waste-heap 9♥ 9♥

Waste-heap J♦ J♦

Fig. 35

Fig. 35 Puss in the Corner
The 2♠ may be built either on the A♠ or A♣.
High cards dealt from the stock should be played on the J♦.

49

Pyramid

Pyramid, or Pile of Twenty-eight, is an interesting patience, and not an easy one. It is said that the player has no better chance of success than about once in 50 games.

Twenty-eight cards are dealt face upwards to the board in seven rows, beginning with a row of one card and increasing each row by one card so that the seventh row will be of seven cards.

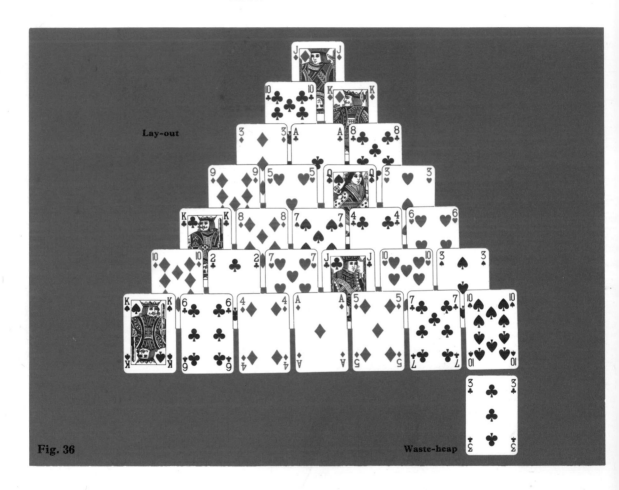

Lay-out

Fig. 36

Waste-heap

Fig. 36 Pyramid
The K ♠ is discarded; the 7 ♣ and 6 ♣ are paired and discarded; the 10 ♠ and 3 ♣ (from the waste-heap) are paired and discarded; the 10 ♦ and 3 ♠ are paired and discarded.
As no further discards are to be made, the next card of the stock is dealt to the waste-heap.
And so on.

The cards should be arranged in the form of a pyramid, so that every card (except those in the bottom row) will be overlapped by two cards in the row below it (*see* Fig. 36). In this way the removal of two adjacent cards in a row will expose the card in the row above it.

The object of the game is to discard the whole pack. Kings are discarded singly, but all other cards are discarded in a pair whose pips add to 13 (a Queen counting as 12 and a Knave as 11). Only exposed cards may be discarded.

50

The stock is turned one card at a time to a waste-heap, the top card of which is exposed and may be paired either with an exposed card in the lay-out or with the next card turned from the stock.

Quadrille

Deal the cards one by one face upwards to a waste-heap. The Aces and 2s, as they are dealt, are played to the centre to serve as foundations, and, by tradition, arranged as shown in Fig. 37.

The object of the game is to build on the foundations

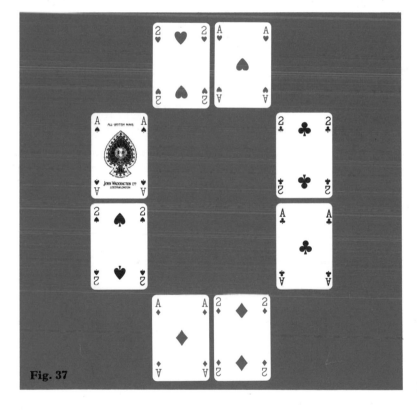

Fig. 37

Fig. 37 Quadrille

broken ascending suit sequences, on the Aces in the order 3.5.7.9.J.K. (odd-numbered cards) and on the 2s in the order 4.6.8.10.Q. (even-numbered cards). Two redeals (three deals in all) are allowed, but the waste-heap must not be shuffled between them.

Success will leave each King with his consort (Queen) on his right, as at the beginning of a quadrille.

A puerile game for when time hangs heavily on one's hands.

51

Raglan

Raglan is an excellent game that is very similar to King Albert (see p. 35) but rather less difficult.

The four Aces are removed from the pack and played to the centre as foundation-cards. Immediately below them, 42 cards are dealt face upwards to the board in a row of nine cards, then eight cards, then seven cards, and so down to a row of three cards. For convenience the cards may overlap. The remaining six cards, known as the reserve, may be held in hand or played face upwards on the board in front of the player (*see* Fig. 38).

The object of the game is to build ascending suit sequences on the Aces to the Kings.

The bottom cards of the columns are exposed. They may be built on a foundation, packed on other exposed cards or

Fig. 38 Raglan

The 2 ♥, from the reserve, is built on the A ♥, and the 3 ♥ on the 2 ♥.

The vacancy is filled with the K ♣, the Q ♥ is packed on the K ♣, the J ♠ on the Q ♥, the 8 ♠ on the 9 ♦ and the 4 ♦ on the 5 ♠.

The 4 ♥ is built on the 3 ♥ and the 5 ♥, from the reserve, on the 4 ♥.

The 7 ♥ is packed on the 8 ♠, and the 8 ♦, from the reserve, on the 9 ♣.

And so on.

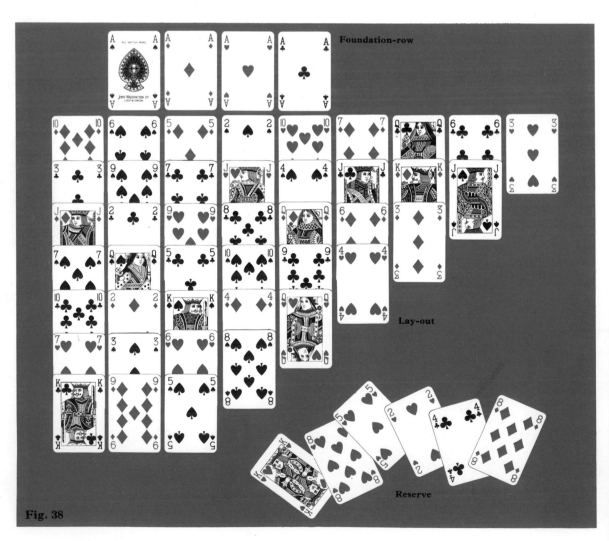

Fig. 38

themselves be packed on, in descending sequences of alternate colour. Only one card may be moved at a time. When all the cards have been moved from a column, the vacancy may be filled with any exposed card. A card in the reserve may be built on a foundation, or packed on an exposed card at the foot of a column; it may not itself be packed on.

Scorpion

Deal to the board a row of seven cards, the first four face downwards, the other three face upwards. Deal two more rows in the same way, and then four rows of seven cards all face upwards. The cards may overlap for convenience. The remaining three cards are set aside face downwards as a heel (*see* Fig. 39).

The object of the game is to build on the four Kings,

Fig. 39 Scorpion
The lay-out is promising.
The 6 ♦ is packed on the 7 ♦, the 9 ♣ on the 10 ♣, the 3 ♥ on the 4 ♥, the Q ♣ on the K ♣, the 7 ♠ on the 8 ♠, the J ♣ with the Q ♦ on the Q ♣, the Q ♦ on the K ♦, the 10 ♣ with the 9 ♣ on the J ♣, the 4 ♥ with the 3 ♥ on the 5 ♥ and the 2 ♥ on the 3 ♥.
The face-downwards card is now cleared and turned face upwards. And so on.

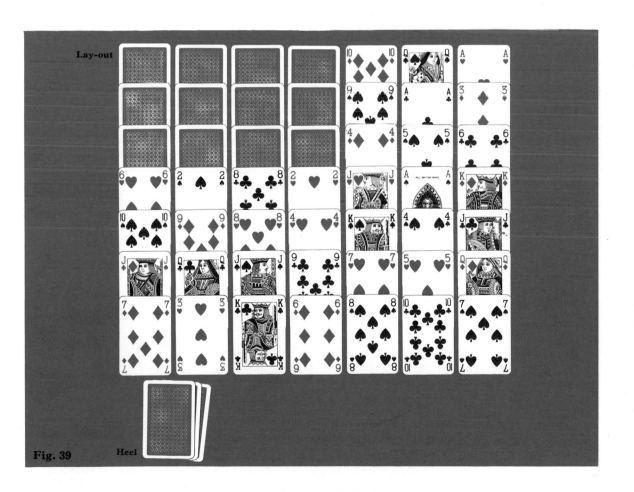

Lay-out

Fig. 39   Heel

53

within the lay-out, descending suit sequences to the Aces.

The cards in the bottom row of the lay-out are exposed and the next lower card of the suit may be packed on them. Nothing, however, may be packed on an Ace. A card may be taken from anywhere in the lay-out, but, when it is, all the other cards below it in the column must be taken with it.

When a face-downwards card is cleared, it is turned face upwards and becomes available. When a column is cleared the vacancy must be filled by a King, together with any cards that may be below it in the column.

When no further moves can be made, the cards in the heel are dealt at the bottom of the three columns at the extreme left of the lay-out.

The game is by no means an easy one and there is not much chance of a player being successful unless every move is first given thought. Careless play will nearly always result in the game being blocked.

The lay-out should be inspected closely, because if there is a reverse sequence in a column, *e.g.* 7, 6, 8 of Clubs, the game can never be won; nor can it be won if there is a criss-cross such as the 8 of Clubs directly on the 3 of Diamonds

Fig. 40 Simple Simon
The Q ♣ may be built on the K ♣, the 10 ♠ may be packed on the J ♠, the 9 ♥ on the 10 ♠, and the 9 ♠ on the 10 ♦.
Now, the 6 ♦ may be packed on the 7 ♥, the 5 ♥ on the 6 ♦, and the vacancy filled with the K ♠.
The Q ♠ may be built on the K ♠, and the vacancy filled with the K ♣ and Q ♣ in sequence.
And so on.

Fig. 40

54

in one column and the 2 of Diamonds on the 9 of Clubs in another. When this occurs it is a waste of time to continue.

If the lay-out looks promising, the first moves should be towards clearing the face-downwards cards.

Simple Simon

Deal the whole pack face upwards to the board in eight rows (which may overlap), the first row of ten cards, the second of nine, and, by decreasing each row by one card, to a row of three cards (*see* Fig. 40).

The object of the game is to build within the lay-out descending suit sequences on exposed Kings to the Aces.

The bottom card of each column (other than a King) may be packed in a descending sequence regardless of suit and colour. Only one card may be moved at a time, except that a sequence may be moved as a whole if it consists of cards all of one suit.

A vacancy left by the removal of all the cards from a column may be filled by any exposed card or by a sequence if all the cards are of one suit.

An excellent game, but the name given to it defeats me because it is far from easy or simple.

Sir Tommy–Lady Betty

No-one knows, and probably no-one ever will know, which is the original patience from which all others were derived. This one, which is sometimes known as Old Patience, may

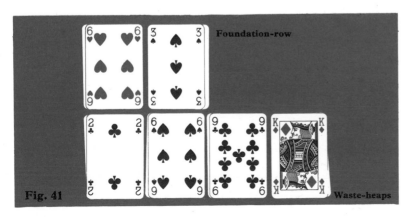

Fig. 41

Foundation-row

Waste-heaps

Fig. 41 Sir Tommy
Two Aces have been played to the foundation-row and subsequently built on.
The next card from the stock is the A ♥; it is played to the foundation-row and the 2 ♣ is built on it.

55

be it. Certainly, the game could hardly be simpler.

The cards are dealt face upwards one by one, and played at the discretion of the player to four waste-heaps (Sir Tommy, *see* Fig. 41) or six (Lady Betty). As they occur, the Aces are played to a foundation-row and there built on in ascending sequences regardless of suits and colour to Kings. The top cards of the waste-heaps are available to be played to the foundations, but as there is only the one deal, and a card may not be transferred from one waste-heap to another, the best that can be done is to reserve one waste-heap on which to play the Kings and hope that they will show up early in the game.

After television, it's the best time-waster known.

Fig. 42 Six by Six
The A ♦ is played to the centre and the 2 ♦ built on it.
The A ♣ is played to the centre.
The 5 ♣ is packed on the 6 ♥.
The J ♥ is packed on the Q ♣, the 10 ♥ on the J ♥, the 9 ♣ on the 10 ♥, the 8 ♠ on the 9 ♣, the 7 ♥ on the 8 ♠ and the 6 ♦ on the 7 ♥.
The A ♥ is played to the centre and the 2 ♥ built on it.
And so on.

Fig. 42

Six by Six

Six by Six is a simple building-up patience that may not be as well known as it deserves to be.

Thirty-six cards are dealt face downwards to the board in six overlapping rows of six cards each (*see* Fig. 42).

The object of the game is to release the Aces and to play them to the centre as foundation-cards; they are then built on in ascending suit sequences to the Kings.

The bottom card of each column is exposed. It may be built on a foundation, packed on an exposed card in the lay-out, or itself be packed on, in descending sequence regardless of suit and colour. Provided the sequential order is retained, a sequence may be moved, either wholly or in part, from the foot of one column to that of another. When all the cards of a column have been played, the vacancy may be filled by any exposed card or by a sequence.

The stock is dealt one card at a time, and any card that cannot be built on a foundation nor packed on the lay-out, is played to the foot of the left-hand column. Only one deal is allowed.

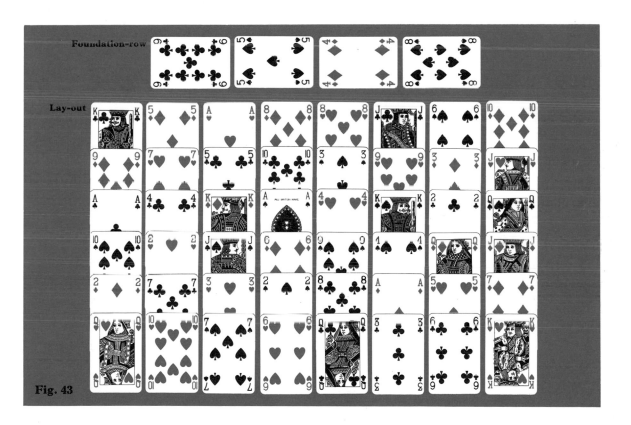

Fig. 43

Fig. 43 Stalactites

The player decides to build on the foundations in twos.
The 10 ♥ is built on the 8 ♠, the Q ♣ on the 10 ♥, the 6 ♥ on the 4 ♦, the 8 ♣ on the 6 ♥ and the 7 ♠ on the 5 ♠.
The J ♦ is now drawn out of the lay-out and built on the 9 ♣, the K ♥ is built on the J ♦ and the 2 ♠ on the K ♥.
And so on.

Stalactites

Stalactites, Old Mole or Grampus, is a fairly simple patience and a rather unusual one.

Deal the first four cards of the pack face upwards to the centre to serve as foundation-cards. It is best to lay them lengthwise so that they can be identified when built on. The remaining 48 cards of the pack are dealt face upwards below them in six rows of eight cards each, which may overlap for convenience (*see* Fig. 43).

After examining the lay-out the player has the option of building an ascending sequence of 13 cards on each foundation either by ones or by twos (*e.g.* . . . 10.J.Q.K.A.2 . . . or . . . 10.Q.A.3.5 . . .). Whichever decision is made applies to all four foundations. The suits are ignored.

The bottom cards of the columns are available for building on the foundations, and any two cards (but not more than two cards) may be drawn out of the lay-out and held in reserve. They may be built on the foundations. If all the cards are moved from a column the vacancy is not filled.

Stone-wall

Deal to the board 36 cards in six rows of six cards each, the first, third and fifth rows face downwards, the second, fourth and sixth rows face upwards. For convenience the rows may overlap. The stock (16 cards in all) may either be held in hand or spread face upwards on the table (*see* Fig. 44).

Any Aces in the stock, or exposed in the sixth row of the layout, are moved to a foundation-row, to be built on in ascending suit sequences up to the Kings.

Exposed cards in the bottom row of the lay-out are packed in descending sequences of alternate colour, either with cards from the stock or exposed cards in the lay-out. A sequence may be transferred either as a whole or in part to an exposed card, provided the card to which the transfer is made is the next higher card in sequence and of alternate colour. When a card or sequence is removed from immediately below a face-downwards card, the card is turned face upwards and is available for play.

When all the cards in a column have been moved, the vacancy may be filled either with an exposed card or sequence from the lay-out, or with a card from the stock.

The game is by no means a difficult one, but success comes only if there is a favourable run of the cards. Vacancies in the top row of the lay-out are very helpful.

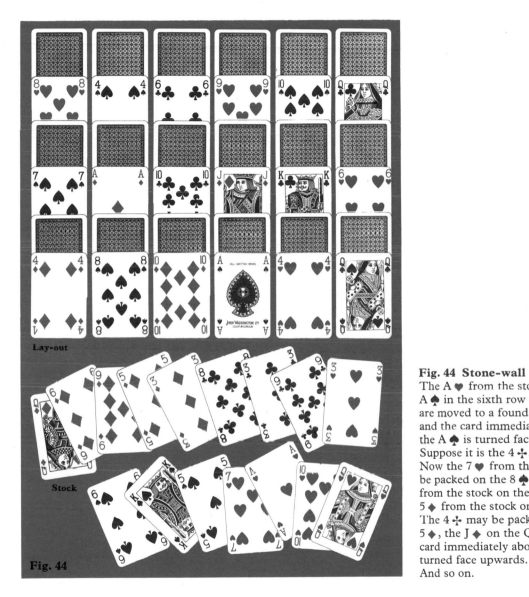

Lay-out

Stock

Fig. 44

Fig. 44 Stone-wall
The A ♥ from the stock and the A ♠ in the sixth row of the lay-out are moved to a foundation-row, and the card immediately above the A ♠ is turned face upwards. Suppose it is the 4 ♣.
Now the 7 ♥ from the stock may be packed on the 8 ♠, the 6 ♠ from the stock on the 7 ♥ and the 5 ♦ from the stock on the 6 ♠. The 4 ♣ may be packed on the 5 ♦, the J ♦ on the Q ♠ and the card immediately above the J ♦ turned face upwards.
And so on.

Tactics

Tactics is one of the older patience games that has attracted to itself many variations. This, I believe, to be the original. Certainly it is by no means the simple, and rather elementary, game that it may seem at first sight.

The whole pack is dealt, one card at a time, face upwards

59

to the board. Aces as they are dealt are played to the centre as foundation-cards. The other 48 cards are distributed among eight waste-heaps, at the discretion of the player (*see* Fig. 45).

When all 52 cards have been dealt, the game is won if the player can build ascending suit sequences on the Aces to the Kings.

Success depends on the way in which the cards are distributed among the eight waste-heaps. Obviously the game cannot be won if a high card is packed on a waste-heap that contains a lower card of the same suit. One waste-heap must

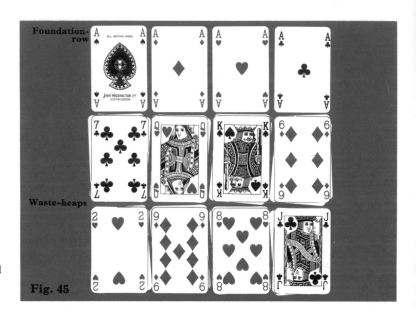

Fig. 45 Tactics
The 2 ♥ is built on the A ♥.
And so on.
In the event the game was blocked because the 4 ♦ was under the 6 ♦.

Fig. 45

be reserved for Kings, another for Queens and a third for Knaves, but once a high card has been played to a waste-heap it is safe to pack a lower card of the same suit on top of it. The low cards are best distributed among the other five waste-heaps, taking the precaution to pack them downwards.

Tower of Hanoy

Remove from the pack the Ace to 9 (inclusive) of any one suit, and, after shuffling them, deal them to the board face upwards in three rows of three cards each (*see* Fig. 46(a)).

The object of the game is to arrange the cards in one column with the 9 at the top descending in sequence to the Ace at the bottom. The movement of the cards is governed by four rules:

1. Only one card may be moved at a time.

Fig. 46(a) Tower of Hanoy
The skilful player will play first to get the 9 at the top of a column. The early moves, therefore, will be: the 2 ♥ below the 9 ♥, the 4 ♥ below the 8 ♥, the 2 ♥ below the 4 ♥, the A ♥ below the 2 ♥ and the 9 ♥ to the middle column (*see* Fig. 46(b)).

Fig. 46(a)

Fig. 46(b)

Fig. 46(b) Tower of Hanoy
With the 9 ♥ in position, the next step is to get the 8 ♥ below it, the 7 ♥ below the 8 ♥, and so on. The moves continue: the A ♥ below the 6 ♥, the 2 ♥ below the 9 ♥, the A ♥ below the 2 ♥, the 4 ♥ below the 6 ♥, etc., etc. Provided the player perseveres, success is assured.

2. Only the bottom card of a column may be moved.

3. A card may be moved only to the bottom of another column and below a higher card.

4. When all the cards in a column have been moved, the vacancy may be filled by the bottom card of either of the other two columns.

Vacancies

Vacancies is more usually known as Gaps, and sometimes as Spaces. Whatever the name, the game is an excellent one with the merit that it is one of the few patience games in which the fortuitous order of the cards is less important than the player's skill. As the player is faced at every move with four vacancies to fill, but can only fill one and whichever move he makes releases another card, much depends on the order in which he fills the vacancies.

The whole pack is dealt face upwards to the board in four rows of 13 cards each, and the Aces are discarded leaving four vacancies (*see* Fig. 47).

The object of the game is to arrange the cards so that every row consists of one suit in sequential order, the 2 on the extreme left and the King on the extreme right. The

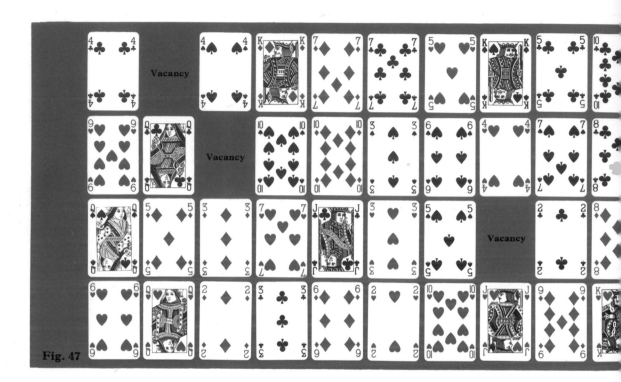

Fig. 47

Fig. 47 Vacancies
The 6 ♠ is played to the right of the 5 ♠, and the 4 ♠ to the right of the 3 ♠.
The 5 ♣ is played to the right of the 4 ♣, and the 6 ♣ to the right of the 5 ♣.
The Q ♠ is played to the right of the J ♠ and the player is now in a position to begin the third row by playing one of the 2s into the vacancy left by the Q ♠.
And so on.

player decides which row he will allocate to each suit, and, having made his decision, must stand by it.

A vacancy may be filled only by the card that is next higher in rank and of the same suit as the card on the left of the vacancy. Obviously, filling a vacancy leaves another vacancy to be filled and this is filled in the same way until the run of the game is brought to a halt by the position of the four Kings.

Three deals are permitted. When no further moves can be made after the first deal, the cards in the lay-out that are out of sequence are picked up, shuffled, and the lay-out remade by dealing the cards to the board with a vacancy in each row to the immediate right of the cards that are in sequence.

Vanbrugh

Remove from the pack the 12 picture cards. Place the four Queens in a fan in the centre of the board, a King and a Knave of the same suit above them, another pair below them and the other pairs one on each side of them (*see* Fig. 48).

The stock is turned one card at a time. The Kings are built on by suit in the order K.A.2.4.6.8.10. and the Knaves by suit in the order J.9.7.5.3. Any card that cannot be built on the lay-out is played to a waste-heap, the top card of which is always available for play.

When a Knave-foundation is built down to a 3 it is ready to be transferred to its King-foundation. The 3 may be built on the King-foundation, however, only if this has been built up to the 2. By transferring the 3 from the Knave-foundation to the King-foundation, the 5 is exposed on the Knave-foundation, and this is moved to the King-foundation only when the King-foundation has been built up to the 4.

In this way success comes when the four King-founda tions have been built up to Knaves, which are given the final accolade of being crowned by their respective Queens.

The waste-heap may be picked up and redealt twice—three deals in all.

Fig. 48 Vanbrugh

Fig. 48

Westcliff

This game is one of the standard patiences that is not too difficult nor too easy. With care the practised player should be able to win eight or nine games out of every 10.

Thirty cards are dealt to the board in three rows of 10 cards each. The first and second row are dealt face downwards, the third row face upwards (*see* Fig. 49(a)). As they

Fig. 49(a)

Fig. 49(a) Westcliff
The A ♦ is played to the centre and the card above it turned face upwards; the 10 ♥ is packed on the J ♣, the 9 ♠ on the 10 ♥, the 5 ♦ on the 6 ♣, and the 4 ♣ on the 5 ♦.
The cards in the second row released by moving the 10 ♥, 9 ♠, 5 ♦ and 4 ♣ are turned face upwards (*see* Fig. 49(b)).

become available, the Aces are played to the centre as foundation-cards, to be built on in ascending suit sequences to the Kings.

The exposed cards of the lay-out may be packed in descending sequences of alternate colour, and any face-upwards card or sequence may be packed on another face-upwards card or sequence in the lay-out, provided that the sequential order is retained. When a face-downwards card is released, by reason of a card or sequence below it being

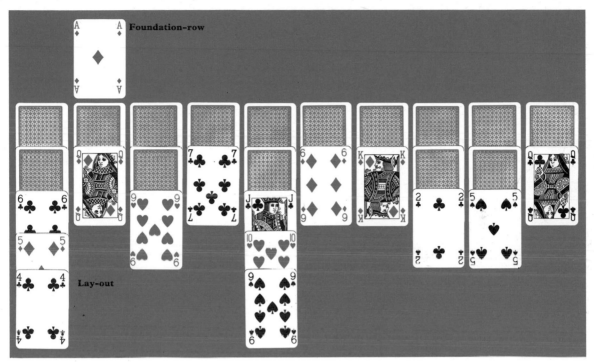

Fig. 49(b)

moved, it is turned face upwards and becomes available.

A vacancy in the lay-out, by reason of all the cards of a column being moved, may be filled either with a card from the waste-heap or with a card or sequence from a column in the lay-out.

The stock is dealt one card at a time and any card that cannot be played to a foundation nor to the lay-out is played to a waste-heap, the top card of which is always available for play. Only one deal is permitted.

Fig. 49(b) Westcliff

Now the 6 ♦ may be packed on the 7 ♣, the 5 ♠ on the 6 ♦, and the Q ♣ on the K ♦.

The cards in the top row released by moving the 6 ♦, 5 ♠ and Q ♣ are turned face upwards.

And so on.

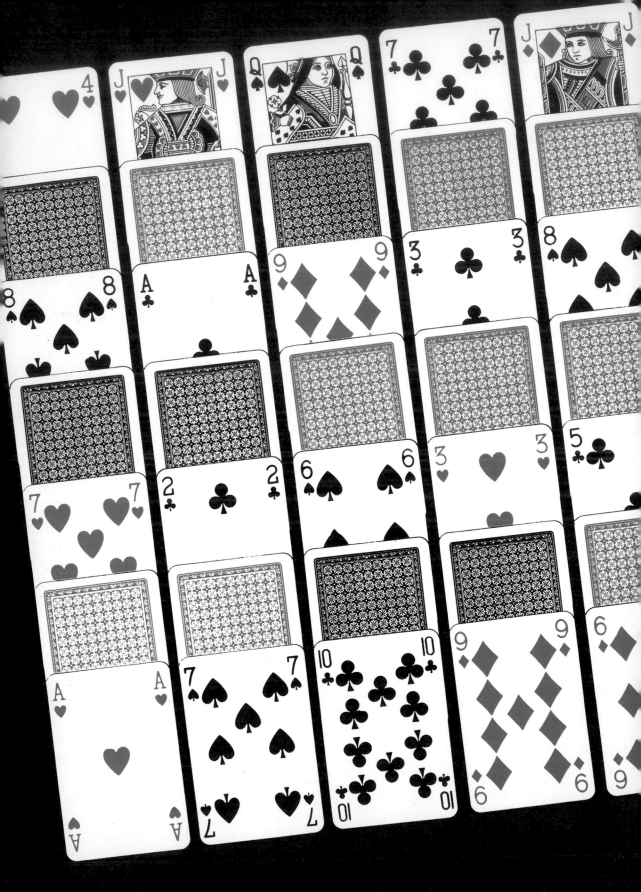

Double-
pack
Games

Above and Below

Deal face upwards to the board eight piles of 11 cards each; then deal face upwards 16 cards, one above and one below each pile (*see* Fig. 50).

The object of the game is to release an Ace and a King of each suit, play them to the centre as foundations, and build ascending suit sequences on the Aces to the Kings, and descending suit sequences on the Kings to the Aces.

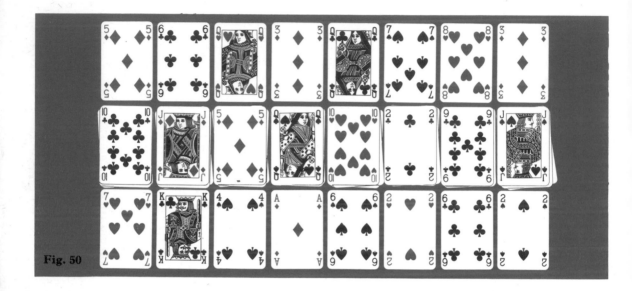

Fig. 50 Above and Below
The A ♦ is played to the foundation-row and the Q ♠ fills the vacancy.
The K ♣ is played to the foundation-row and the vacancy is filled by the J ♦, the Q ♣ is built on the K ♣ and the vacancy filled with the 10 ♥.
The 7 ♥ is packed on the 8 ♥, the 10 ♣ fills the vacancy and the 9 ♣ is packed on the 10 ♣.
The 7 ♠ is packed on the 6 ♠ and the 2 ♣ fills the vacancy.
And so on.

The top cards of the piles are available to be built on the foundations, or packed on the cards in the rows, either in ascending or descending suit sequences, the direction of which may be reversed at the option of the player. The cards in the rows are available to be built on the foundations or packed on each other in ascending or descending suit sequences. Cards may be moved only singly, not in sequences.

A vacancy in a row must be filled by the top card of the pile immediately above or below it, and when all the cards of a pile have been played, the vacancy must be filled by the top card of the pile on its right or left.

Alhambra

Remove one Ace of each suit and one King of each suit and play them to the centre as foundation-cards. Below them

68

deal face upwards 32 cards in eight packets of four cards each (*see* Fig. 51).

The object of the game is to build ascending suit sequences on the Aces to the Kings, and descending suit sequences on the Kings to the Aces.

The stock is dealt one card at a time and any card that cannot be built on a foundation is played to a waste-heap, the top card of which is available to be built on a foundation.

The top cards of the eight packets are available to be built on the foundations, or they may be packed on the top card of the waste-heap either in ascending or in descending,

Fig. 51 Alhambra
The Q ♦ is built on the K ♦, and the 2 ♠ on the A ♠.
The player has the option of packing either the 10 ♥ or the 8 ♥ on the 9 ♥, the top card of the waste-heap.
And so on.

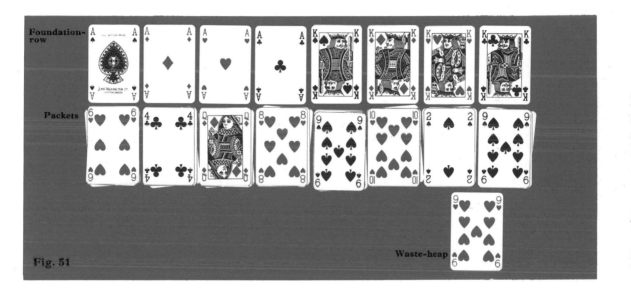

Fig. 51

round-the-corner suit sequences. A vacancy made by playing all four cards of a packet is not filled.

The stock may be dealt three times in all.

Alternation

Forty-nine cards are dealt to the board in seven overlapping rows of seven cards each: the first, third, fifth and seventh rows face upwards, the second, fourth and sixth face downwards (*see* Fig. 52).

The object of the game is to release the eight Aces, play them to the centre as foundation-cards and build on them ascending suit sequences to the Kings.

The bottom cards of the columns are exposed. They may be built on the foundations, packed on other exposed cards in the lay-out, or be themselves packed on, in descending sequences of alternate colour. Provided the sequential

Fig. 52

Stock

Fig. 52 Alternation
The A ♥ is played to the
foundation-row; the 9 ♦ is packed
on the 10 ♣ and the 8 ♣ on the
9 ♦; the 6 ♦ is packed on the 7 ♠.
The face-downwards cards are
turned face upwards.
And so on.

order is retained, a column may be moved, either as a whole
or in part, from one column to another. When the play of a
card or sequence results in a face-downwards card occurring
at the bottom of a column it is turned face upwards. A
vacancy may be filled by any exposed card or sequence.

The stock is dealt one card at a time, and any card that
cannot be built on a foundation nor packed on the lay-out
is played to a waste-heap. There is only one deal.

Babette

Deal face upwards to the board a row of eight cards, below
it another row, and so on, until the pack is exhausted. After
dealing a row, however, and before dealing the next, play
all available cards to a foundation-row. The object of the
game is to play one Ace and one King of each suit to a
foundation-row, and build ascending suit sequences on
the Aces to the Kings, and descending suit sequences on the
Kings to the Aces.

A card is exposed and available to be played to a founda-

70

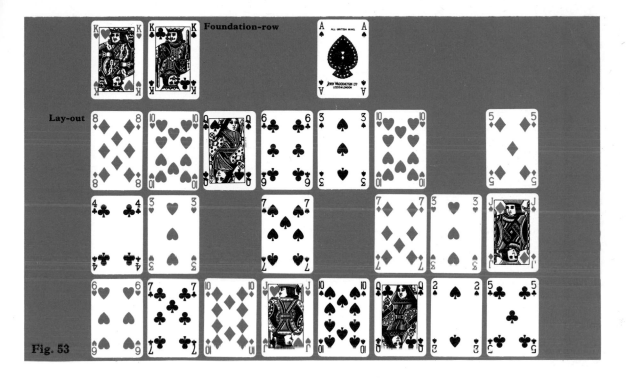

Fig. 53

tion when its lower edge is free. No other card is available to be played, and vacancies that occur by playing cards from the rows to the foundations are not filled (*see* Fig. 53).

One redeal is allowed. When the stock is exhausted, the cards remaining in each column are slid into packets, which are picked up from left to right to remake the pack.

Unless it is necessary to release important cards, it is very unwise to play a card from above a vacancy until its duplicate has been dealt; between duplicates the game is often lost if the right card is not chosen to be played.

Fig. 53 Babette

The Q ♠, 3 ♠ and all eight cards in the third row are exposed.

The 2 ♠ may be built on the A ♠, but the 3 ♠ should not be built on the 2 ♠; it is better to wait until the other 3 ♠ is dealt.

The Q ♣ should be built on the K ♣.

And so on.

Big Bertha

Deal face upwards to the board 90 cards in six overlapping rows of 15 cards each. The remaining 14 cards are retained in hand, or spread on the table in front of the player, as a reserve (*see* Fig. 54).

The object of the game is to release the Aces, play them to the centre as foundation-cards and build ascending suit sequences on them to the Queens (Big Berthas). As they

71

become exposed the Kings are taken out of the game.

The bottom cards of the columns and the cards in the reserve are exposed and available to be built on the foundations. The bottom cards of the columns may also be packed on each other in descending sequences of alternate colour. Provided the sequential order and alternation of colour are retained a sequence may be moved from the foot of one column to another.

A vacancy in the lay-out, when all the cards of a column have been played, may be filled with a sequence or an exposed card.

Blockade

Deal face upwards to the board a row of 12 cards. Any Aces are played to the centre as foundation-cards (to be built on in ascending suit sequences to the Kings) and any sequence-cards are built on the foundations. The cards in the row may be packed on each other in descending suit sequences, which may be moved from one exposed card to another, so long as the sequential order is retained (*see* Fig. 55).

When all building and packing has been done, the vacancies in the lay-out are filled from the stock, and building, packing and filling of vacancies is continued.

When no further moves are to be made, successive rows of 12 cards are dealt until the stock is exhausted, the player pausing between each deal to build on the foundations, pack on the lay-out and fill any vacancies.

British Square

British Square is a building patience with the unusual feature that the foundations are built first in ascending sequences and then in descending ones.

Sixteen cards are dealt face upwards to the board in four overlapping rows of four cards each. As they become available an Ace of each suit is played to the centre to serve as foundations. They are built on in ascending suit sequences to the Kings, then the duplicate Kings are placed on the foundations and built on in descending suit sequences to the Aces.

The bottom card of a column is available to be built on a foundation or may be packed on either in ascending or descending suit sequence. The first card packed on a column dictates the direction of a sequence, which cannot be

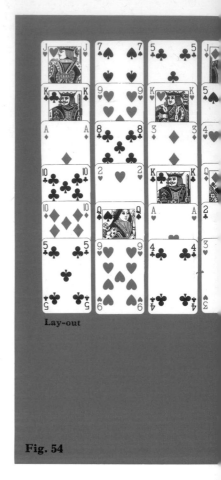

Lay-out

Fig. 54

Fig. 54 Big Bertha

Take the K ♥ and K ♦ out of the game.

Play the A ♦, A ♠ and A ♣ to the centre.

Build the 2 ♠ on the A ♠ and the 2 ♣ on the A ♣.

Pack the 5 ♦ on the 6 ♠ and take the K ♠ out of the game.

Pack the 4 ♣ on the 5 ♦.

Play the A ♥ to the centre and take the K ♣ out of the game.

And so on.

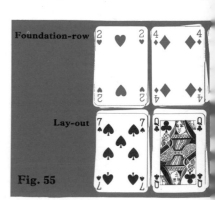

Foundation-row

Lay-out

Fig. 55

72

Reserve

reversed by later cards. Only one card, however, may be moved at a time, so the player may alter the direction of a sequence by reversing it onto an available card at the foot of another column. An ascending sequence ends with a King, a descending one with an Ace. A vacancy is filled either by a card from the stock or from the waste-heap (*see* Fig. 56).

The stock is turned one card at a time, and any card that cannot be built on a foundation nor packed on the lay-out is played to a waste-heap, the top card of which is always

Fig. 55 Blockade
During the deals the Ace-foundations have been built up.
The 4 ♠ is built on the 3 ♠, the J ♣ is packed on the Q ♣ and the 9 ♥ on the 10 ♥.
And so on.

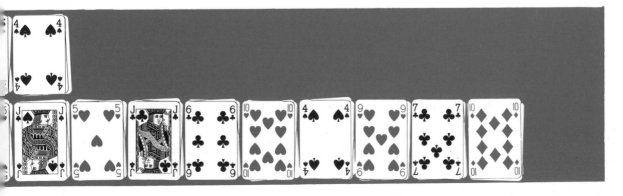

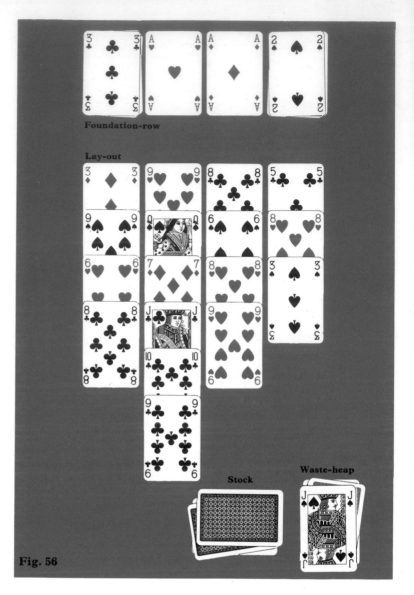

Foundation-row

Lay-out

Stock

Waste-heap

Fig. 56

Fig. 56 British Square

The Aces have been played to the
centre as foundation-cards,
the A ♣ built up to the 3 ♣, and
the A ♠ to the 2 ♠.
The 8 ♣ is packed on the 9 ♣
because the 10 ♣ packed on the
J ♣ dictates a descending
sequence.
The 3 ♠ is built on the 2 ♠,
releasing the 8 ♥.
The 8 ♥, however, may not be
packed on the 9 ♥ because the 9 ♥
packed on the 8 ♥ dictates an
ascending sequence.
And so on.

available to be played. There is no second deal.

Do not forget that the foundations are first built on in
ascending sequences and then in descending ones. As a
result, a duplicate card in the lay-out should be packed on in
the opposite direction.

Capricious

Play to the centre as foundations an Ace and a King of each
suit. Below them deal, face upwards to the board, 12 cards.
They may be arranged in any way that is convenient to the
player; three rows of four cards each is as good as any (*see*
Fig. 57).

74

Fig. 57 Capricious
The foundations have been built
up during the deal.
The 2 ♠ is packed on the A ♠ and
the 2 ♣ on the 3 ♣ or, if preferred,
the 3 ♣ on the 2 ♣.
The cards under those that have
been moved are available to be
played.
And so on.

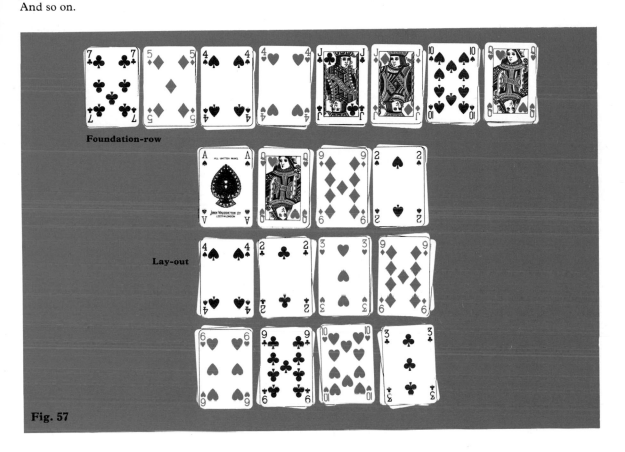

Foundation-row

Lay-out

Fig. 57

The object of the game is to build ascending suit sequences on the Aces to the Kings, and descending suit sequences on the Kings to the Aces.

Cards in the lay-out may be built on the foundations as they are dealt, and the vacancies filled with cards from the stock. Twelve cards from the stock are then dealt on top of those in position. Any available card is played to a foundation when dealt and its place in the lay-out filled by the next card from the stock; cards already played to the lay-out may not be subsequently built on a foundation. When the whole pack has been dealt, the top cards of the 12 piles are available not only to be built on the foundations but to be packed on each other in ascending or descending suit sequences. Sequences in the lay-out are not round-the-corner (only a Queen may be packed on a King and a 2 on an Ace) but it is

75

permitted to reverse the direction of a sequence on the same pile.

Two redeals are allowed. To remake the pack, the piles are picked up in the reverse order to which they are dealt.

Fig. 58 The Clock
The J ♣ is built on the 10 ♣, the 10 ♦ on the 9 ♦ and the J ♦ on the 10 ♦.
The 5 ♠ is built on the 4 ♠, the 7 ♣ on the 6 ♣, the 6 ♠ on the 5 ♠ and the 8 ♥ on the 7 ♥.
The 9 ♥ is built on the 8 ♥ and the 10 ♥ on the 9 ♥.
And so on.

The Clock

The Clock, Big Ben or Grandfather's Clock, is a first-class game and the player has a chance of winning one out of every two attempts. To be successful, however, foresight and ingenuity are necessary.

Fig. 58

76

A 2 of Clubs, 3 of Hearts, 4 of Spades, 5 of Diamonds, 6 of Clubs, 7 of Hearts, 8 of Spades, 9 of Diamonds, 10 of Clubs, Knave of Hearts, Queen of Spades and King of Diamonds are removed from the pack to serve as foundations. They are placed on the board in a circle corresponding to the hours on the dial of a clock; the 2 of Clubs at nine o'clock and so in sequence to the King of Diamonds at eight o'clock. The lay-out is completed with 36 cards dealt about the dial of the clock in 12 fans of three cards each (*see* Fig. 58).

The object of the game is to build ascending, round-the-corner suit sequences on the foundation-cards until each reaches the correct hour on the clock.

The top card of each fan is exposed. It may be built on a foundation, packed on the top card of another fan or itself be packed on, in a descending, round-the-corner suit sequence. When all plays have been made, the fans are filled from the stock, because a fan must be maintained at a minimum of three cards. They must be filled from the stock and in rotation beginning at one o'clock.

The stock is dealt one card at a time, and any card that cannot be built on a foundation nor packed on a fan is played to a waste-heap. The top card of the waste-heap is available at any time to be built on a foundation: it must not be packed on a fan nor used to fill one.

Colorado

Colorado is a fairly simple game that should succeed about five times out of six.

Deal face upwards to the board 20 cards in two rows of 10 cards each. As they become available, play to the centre

Fig. 59 Colorado
The A ♠, A ♣ and K ♦ have been played to the foundation-row; the other K ♦ may not be used as a foundation-card.
The 2 ♠ may be built on the A ♠ and the 3 ♠ on the 2 ♠.
And so on.

Fig. 59

77

one Ace and one King of each suit (*see* Fig. 59).

The object of the game is to build ascending suit sequences on the Aces to the Kings, and descending suit sequences on the Kings to the Aces.

The stock is dealt one card at a time and any card that cannot be played to a foundation is played to one of the 20 cards in the lay-out, which, in reality, are so many waste-heaps. The top cards of the waste-heaps are available to be played to the foundations, and, when all the cards of a waste-heap have been played, the vacancy is filled with a card from the stock.

A card must not be played from one waste-heap to another, nor must a card be dealt from the stock until the previous one has been placed.

Fig. 60(a)

Fig. 60(a) Congress
The A ♦ is played to the centre and since, as yet, there is no waste-heap the vacancy is filled from the stock.
The 5 ♦ is packed on the 6 ♠ and the vacancy filled from the stock. And so on.

Fig. 60(b) Congress
The Q ♦ is packed on the K ♥. The player may look at the next card of the stock and decide whether to fill the vacancy with it or with the 5 ♣. And so on.

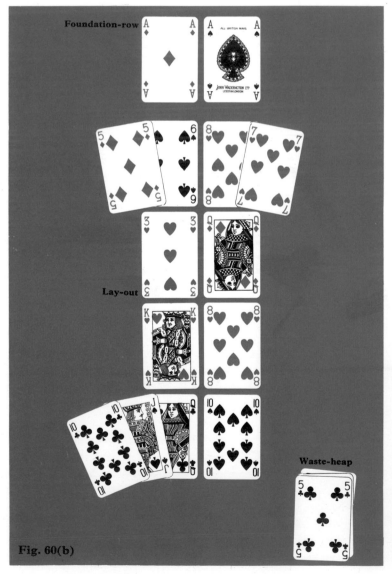

Foundation-row

Lay-out

Waste-heap

Fig. 60(b)

78

Congress

Deal face upwards to the board eight cards in two columns of four cards each (*see* Fig. 60(a)).

The object of the game is to play the eight Aces—as they become available—to the centre and build on them ascending suit sequences to the Kings.

The cards in the lay-out are packed in descending sequences regardless of suit and colour. Only one card may be moved at a time. The stock is turned one card at a time, and a card that cannot be packed on the lay-out nor built on a foundation is played to a waste-heap, the top card of which is available to be played. A vacancy in the lay-out must be filled at once either from the stock or the waste-heap: it is permitted to look at the next card from the stock before deciding whether to fill a vacancy with it or the top card of the waste-heap (*see* Fig. 60(b)).

Corner Stones

The lay-out of Corner Stones, or Four Corners, is very simple. Deal face upwards to the board 12 cards in two columns of six cards each, with sufficient room between them to allow for two columns of foundation-cards. The top and bottom cards of the two columns are turned horizontally (*see* Fig. 61).

As they become available an Ace and a King of each suit are arranged in two columns in the centre, the Ace and King of the same suit being placed side by side. The object of the game is to build ascending suit sequences on the Aces to the Kings, and descending suit sequences on the Kings to the Aces.

The stock is turned one card at a time to cover in turn the cards already in position, and any card that may be played to a foundation is subject to the restriction that if it would fall on one of the horizontal cards it may be played to any foundation, but if it would fall on a card in the vertical columns it may be played only to a foundation in the same row. The horizontal cards and those in the columns must not be deprived of cards, and when a card is played to a foundation the next card in the stock is dealt to cover the appropriate card in the lay-out.

When the stock has been dealt, the restriction is lifted. The top cards of the 12 piles in the lay-out are exposed. They may be built on any foundation, packed on other exposed

79

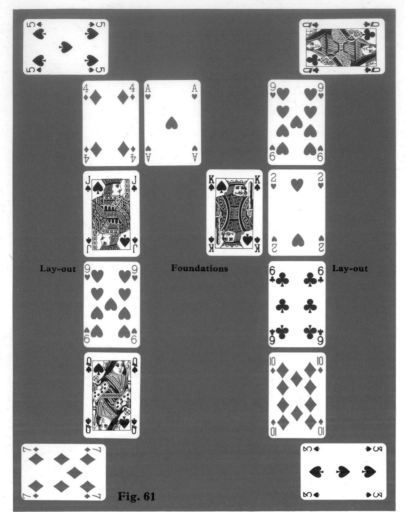

Fig. 61 Corner Stones

The A ♥ and K ♠ were played to the foundation-centre during the deal and their places filled by cards from the stock.

The Q ♠ and 2 ♥ cannot be built on the foundations because they were dealt to the wrong rows. And so on.

Fig. 61

cards or themselves be packed on in ascending, or descending, round-the-corner sequences, regardless of suit and colour.

When the top cards of two foundations of the same suit are in sequence, one may be reversed on the other, with the exception of the Ace or King foundation-cards.

Two redeals are allowed. The cards in the lay-out are picked up in the same order as they are dealt and redealt without shuffling.

Even though the player has three deals in all it is not an easy game, and to be successful the player must make the most of reversing sequences.

Cromwell

The late Mr Charles Jewell composed a number of double-pack patiences: this is one of his best.

Fig. 62 Cromwell

The 4 ♣ is built on the 3 ♣, the 8 ♠ on the 7 ♠ and the A ♦ is played to the foundation-row.

The 2 ♦, 3 ♦, 4 ♦, 5 ♦ and 6 ♦ are built on the A ♦, and the 7 ♣, 8 ♣, 9 ♣, 10 ♣ and J ♣ on the 6 ♣.

The 7 ♥ and 6 ♥ are packed on the 8 ♥, the Q ♠ on the K ♠ and the J ♠ and 10 ♠ on the Q ♠. And so on.

80

Foundation-row

Lay-out

Fig. 62

The whole pack is dealt face upwards to the board in 26 fans of four cards each. Aces, when they become available, are played to the centre as foundation-cards, to be built up to the Kings in ascending suit sequences. The top cards of the fans are exposed: they may be built on the foundations, packed on other exposed cards or be themselves packed on, in descending suit sequences. A sequence may be moved from one exposed card to another either in part or as a whole, provided that the sequential order is retained. Vacancies in the lay-out, when all the cards of a fan have been moved, are not filled (*see* Fig. 62).

As a result of vacancies not being filled, it is clear that the game cannot be won unless at least one King is dealt at the bottom of a fan. The player, therefore, has the grace of interchanging any two cards once at any stage of the game.

Success depends very largely on looking ahead before making a move. It is essential to take note of the positions occupied by the Kings. The game is likely to be an easy one, and success assured, if two or more Kings are at the bottom of fans. By contrast, the game will prove a difficult one, calling for consideration before a move is made, if two or three Kings are near the top of their fans. Until those Kings are played (and they can only be played as the last card to a foundation) the lower cards under them are immobilized, and the player must direct his moves towards releasing the duplicates of the immobilized cards. Every effort should be made towards building cards on the foundations, because any card that can be built on a foundation is not pulling its weight if left in the lay-out.

Diamond

Diamond offers the player little opportunity to exhibit his skill, but it is an interesting game, leisurely, with an attractive lay-out.

Forty-one cards are dealt face upwards to the board in nine rows, the first and last each of one card, the second and eighth of three cards, the third and seventh of five cards, the fourth and sixth of seven cards and the fifth of nine cards (*see* Fig. 63).

The object of the game is to play all eight Aces (when they become available) to the centre, and build on them ascending suit sequences to the Kings.

The cards in the lay-out are not packed on: they may be used only for building on the foundations, and the player is restricted to moving only those cards with at least one free side–the top and bottom of a card do not count as its sides.

Fig. 63 Diamond
The A ♥ is played to the centre and the 2 ♥ built on it.
The A ♠ is played to the centre and the 2 ♠ built on it.
The A ♣ is played to the centre and the 2 ♣ built on it.
The player has the option of building on the 2 ♠ either the 3 ♠ in the third row or that in the seventh row; he will choose the latter because it frees the 3 ♥ that is built on the 2 ♥.
And so on.

Fig. 63

83

The stock is dealt one card at a time, and any card that cannot be played to a foundation must be played to one or other of three waste-heaps, which are fed in turn from left to right. The top card of a waste-heap is available to be played to a foundation, and if two cards are available to be played to the same foundation, the player may play either.

When the stock is exhausted the player fills any vacancies in the lay-out with the cards that have been played to the left-hand waste-heap. If there are not enough cards in it to fill all the vacancies, cards are taken from the middle waste-heap, and from the right-hand one if necessary. The player may pick out the cards to fill the vacancies, but he must not play any to a foundation.

When the lay-out has been filled, the cards remaining in the waste-heaps are shuffled and dealt.

A third deal is permitted under the same rules. When this deal has been completed, however, if the game has not been won, the cards remaining in the lay-out and in the waste-heaps are shuffled together and a fourth (and final) deal played with a lay-out of 25 cards; namely a diamond of seven rows, the first and last each of one card, the second and sixth of three cards, the third and fifth of five cards and the fourth of seven cards.

This second diamond should result in the game being successful, but there is no guarantee.

Diavolo

Deal face downwards to the board 45 cards in nine overlapping rows, the first of nine cards, the second of eight cards, the third of seven cards, and so to a row of only one card. Turn face upwards the bottom card of each column (see Fig. 64).

The object of the game is to release two black Aces and two red Aces, play them to the centre as foundation-cards and build on them ascending colour sequences to the Kings; simultaneously, to pack within the lay-out descending sequences of alternate colour on two black Kings to black Aces and on two red Kings to red Aces.

The face-upwards cards at the foot of the columns are available to be built on the foundations, packed on other exposed cards in the lay-out, or themselves be packed on, in descending sequences of alternate colour. A sequence may be moved either wholly or in part from one exposed card to another, so long as the sequential order and colour alternation is retained; and when a complete sequence from King to Ace has been packed in the lay-out, it is taken out of the game. When a card is moved from the foot of a column, the face-downwards card immediately above it is turned face up-wards and becomes available for play.

A vacancy in the lay-out, when all the cards of a column have been played or a complete sequence removed, is filled either with a King or a sequence headed by a King.

The stock is turned one card at a time, and any card that cannot be built on a foundation nor packed on the lay-out is played to a waste-heap, the top card of which is always available to be played.

The game ends when the stock is exhausted.

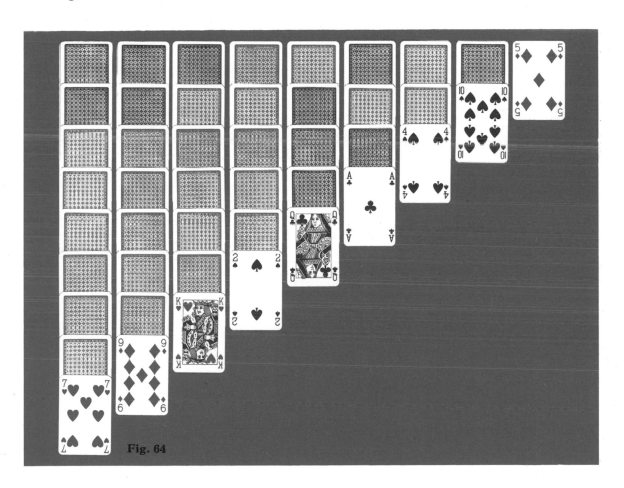

Fig. 64

Diavolo is far from an easy game, and success is rare. It is well named. Good judgement is essential because building ascending sequences on the foundations clashes with packing descending sequences on the Kings in the lay-out. All the time the player has to decide whether a card should be built on an Ace-sequence or packed on a King-sequence, and sometimes it is best to do neither and leave the card where it is, to help towards clearing a column later in the game.

Fig. 64 Diavolo
The A ♣ is played to the centre and the 2 ♠ built on it.
The Q ♣ is packed on the K ♥, the 9 ♦ on the 10 ♠ and the 4 ♠ on the 5 ♦.
And so on.

85

The comparatively large number of face-downwards cards in the three columns on the left of the lay-out usually present difficulties. Every effort should be made to reduce their number, even at the cost of foregoing other plays.

A complete King to Ace sequence within the lay-out should not be taken out of the game at once. By leaving it in the game it may prove useful to split in order to reach face-downwards cards in the lay-out.

Dieppe

Fig. 65 Dieppe
The 2 ♣ and 2 ♦ and 3 ♦ were played to the foundation-row during the deal.
The J ♥ is packed on the Q ♣, the 8 ♥ on the 9 ♦, the 7 ♣ on the 8 ♥, the 5 ♥ on the 6 ♠, the 10 ♠ on the J ♥ and the 4 ♠ on the 5 ♥
The vacancy is filled by the Q ♣ with the J ♥ and 10 ♠.
And so on.

Remove the Aces from the pack and play them to the centre as foundation-cards, on which to build ascending suit sequences to the Kings.

Below them deal face upwards to the board a row of eight cards, playing any to a foundation and filling the vacancy with a card from the stock. Deal a second row and a third row in the same way. For convenience the cards in the rows may overlap (*see* Fig. 65).

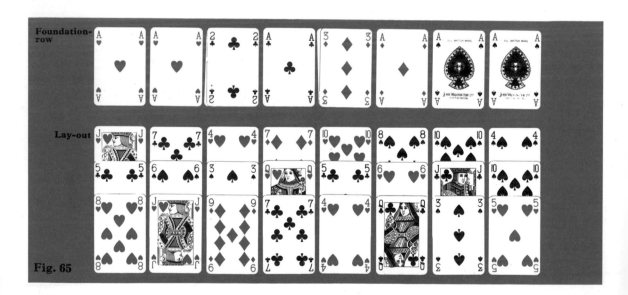

Fig. 65

The cards in the bottom row of the lay-out are exposed and may be built on a foundation, packed on other exposed cards or be themselves packed on, in descending sequences irrespective of suit and colour. A sequence may be moved either in whole or in part from one exposed card to another, so long as the sequential order is retained. If all the cards of a column are moved, the vacancy may be filled by any exposed card or sequence of cards.

The stock is dealt one card at a time and any card that

cannot be built on a foundation, nor packed on the lay-out, is played to a waste-heap, the top card of which is always available. There is no second deal.

Diplomat

Deal face upwards to the board eight fans of four cards each (*see* Fig. 66). As they become available play the eight Aces to a foundation-row, to be built on in ascending suit sequences to the Kings.

The exposed cards of the fans are available to be built on the foundations, packed on other exposed cards in the lay-out and be themselves packed on, in descending sequences

Fig. 66 Diplomat
The 8 ♠ is packed on the 9 ♦, and the 10 ♥ on the J ♠.
The 7 ♦ is packed on the 8 ♠ and the 6 ♥ on the 7 ♦.
The 2 ♣ is packed on the 3 ♠, the vacancy filled by the 4 ♣ and the A ♥ is played to the foundation-row.
The J ♠ with the 10 ♥ is packed on the Q ♥, and the A ♣ is played to the foundation-row.
And so on.

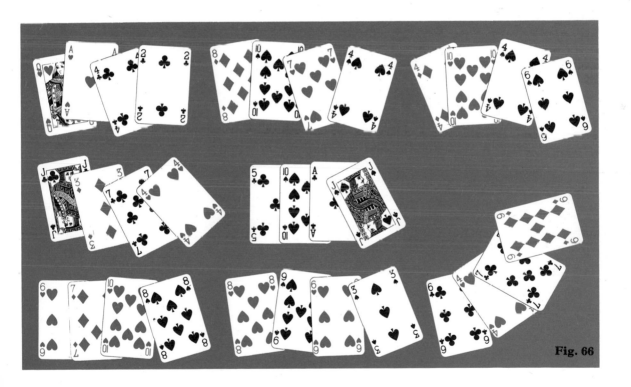

Fig. 66

regardless of suit and colour. Sequences and part-sequences may be moved from one fan to another, provided the sequential order is retained.

A vacancy made by clearing a fan may be filled by any available card.

The stock is dealt one card at a time, and any card that cannot be played to a foundation nor to the lay-out is played to a waste-heap, the top card of which is available to be played.

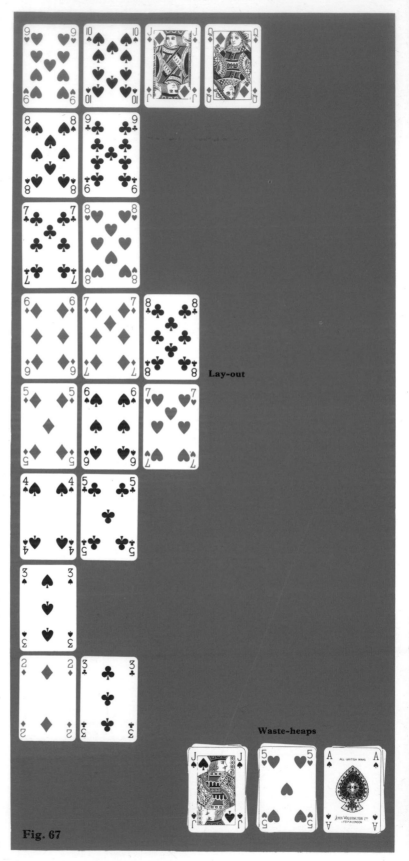

Lay-out

Waste-heaps

Fig. 67 Display

Fig. 67

88

Display

An interesting and a unique game that calls for more watch-fulness than skill.

Deal the top card of the pack face upwards to the left of the board. Continue to deal one card at a time and any card that cannot be played to the lay-out is played to one or other of three waste-heaps, at the discretion of the player. We will suppose that the first card dealt is the 9 of Hearts. When the 10 of any suit is dealt it is played to the right of the 9, and when the Knave of any suit is dealt it is played to the right of the 10. An 8 is played below the 9, and a 7 below the 8. And so on.

The object of the game is to arrange the whole pack in round-the-corner sequences, regardless of suit and colour, in eight rows (*see* Fig. 67).

No card may be played to the lay-out unless the previous one is in position, but the top cards of the waste-heaps are always available to be played.

When the pack is exhausted the waste-heaps are gathered and redealt, this time with only one waste-heap. There is no third deal.

It helps towards success to keep the eight rows as nearly as possible to the same length, and not to play too many cards of one rank to the same waste-heap.

Dog

Remove from the pack an Ace and a King of each suit, and play them to the centre as foundation-cards. The Aces are built on in ascending suit sequences to the Kings, the Kings in descending suit sequences to the Aces.

Deal the rest of the pack face upwards to the board in 13 piles. As the cards are dealt, call 'Ace' as a card is played to the first pile, 'Two' for the second, and so to 'Knave' for the eleventh pile, 'Queen' for the twelfth, and 'King' for the thirteenth. Whenever there is a coincidence the card is not played to the pile, but put aside face downwards to a heel, and the next card of the pack dealt to the pile in its place (*see* Fig. 68).

The top cards of the piles are exposed and, when the whole pack has been dealt, but not before, are available to be built

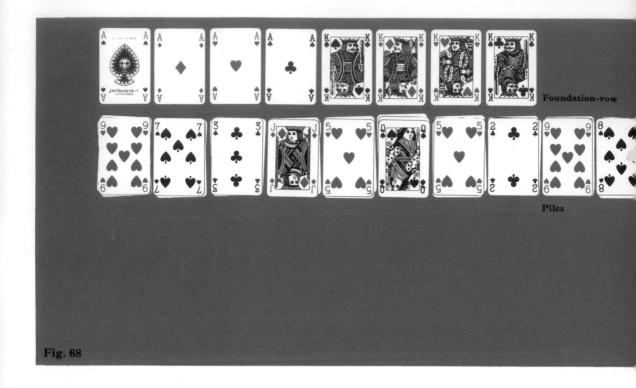

Fig. 68

on the foundations. When a card is taken off a pile the one immediately under it becomes available for play.

When all plays have been made, the top card of the heel is taken up and is available to be built on a foundation; if it cannot be played immediately the pile whose number corresponds to that of the card is taken in hand and sorted. Cards in correct sequence are built on the foundations; the others may be arranged in any order that the player chooses. The pile is replaced on the board, but horizontally to show that it has been sorted, because a pile may be sorted only once. If a second card of the same rank is drawn from the heel, the player may lift and sort any pile that has not already been picked up.

In turn each card in the heel is treated in the same way, and if any cards are left in the heel after all the piles have been sorted, they are turned face upwards and available to be built on the foundations.

Two redeals are allowed. Piles 1 to 6 are picked up in this order, pile 13 and any cards left in the heel are placed on top of them, and piles 12 to 7 are picked up in this order and placed on top of the pack. The redeals are dealt and played in the same way as the first deal.

At any time during the play any card that is in sequence and of the same suit may be transferred from an Ace-foundation to a King-foundation, or *vice-versa*.

Fig. 68 Dog

The 2 ♣ is built on the A ♣, the 3 ♣ on the 2 ♣ and the 2 ♦ on the A ♦.

The Q ♠ is built on the K ♠ and the Q ♥ on the K ♥.

And so on.

Fig. 69 Eight by Eight

The 9 ♦ is packed on the 10 ♠, the 10 ♠ with the 9 ♦ on the J ♥ and the 8 ♥ on the 9 ♦.

The 4 ♣ is packed on the 5 ♦, the A ♥ is played to the centre and the 2 ♥ built on the A ♥.

The 5 ♦ with the 4 ♣ is packed on the 6 ♠ and the 6 ♠ with the 5 ♦ and the 4 ♣, on the 7 ♣.

The A ♠ is played to the centre. And so on.

90

Eight by Eight

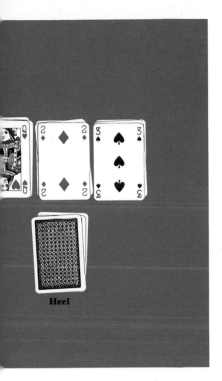

Heel

Eight by Eight is a simple, but nonetheless interesting, building-up patience.

Sixty-four cards are dealt face upwards to the board in eight overlapping rows of eight cards each (*see* Fig.69).

The object of the game is to release the eight Aces, play them to the centre as foundation-cards, and build on them ascending suit sequences to the Kings.

The bottom card of a column is exposed. It may be built on a foundation, packed on another exposed card, or itself be packed on, in a descending sequence regardless of suit and colour. A sequence may be moved from one column to another either as a whole or in part, but a vacancy, when all the cards of a column have been moved, may be filled only with a suit sequence or a single, exposed card.

The stock is dealt in bundles of three cards to a waste-heap; if at the end of the stock there are less than three cards, they are dealt singly. If a redeal is necessary the waste-heap is picked up and dealt two cards at a time, and if another redeal is necessary, the cards are dealt singly. No more than two redeals are allowed. The top card of the waste-heap is always available to be played.

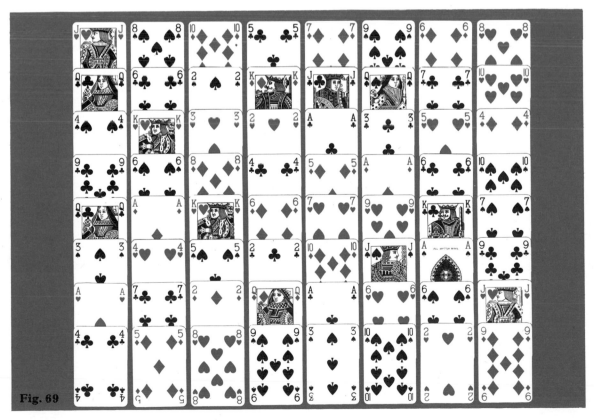

Fig. 69

91

Fig. 70 The Emperor
The 4 ♥ is packed on the 5 ♠, the 3 ♠ from the foundation on the 4 ♥, the 2 ♦ on the 3 ♠ and the top card of the sealed packet above the 2 ♦ brought into play.
The 7 ♦ is packed on the 8 ♠ and the top card of the sealed packet above the 7 ♦ brought into play.
The 6 ♠ with the 5 ♦ are packed on the 7 ♦ and the top card of the sealed packet above the 6 ♠ brought into play.
And so on.

The Emperor

The Emperor is a patience that lends itself to forethought and much ingenuity.

Deal to the board 30 cards face downwards in 10 packets of three cards each; they are known as the sealed packets and, below each, deal a card face upwards. Aces, as they occur, are played to the centre as foundation-cards, to be built on in ascending suit sequences to the Kings (*see* Fig. 70).

The 10 cards below the sealed packets are available to be

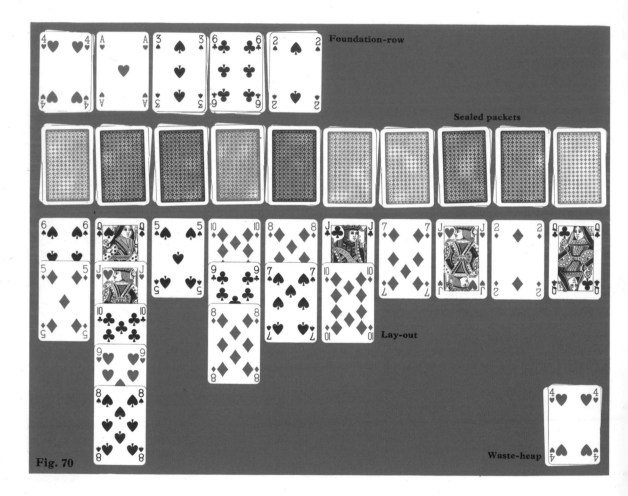

Fig. 70

packed with cards dealt from the stock, and may themselves be packed on each other, in descending sequences of alternate colour. Sequences and part-sequences may be moved from one column to another, provided the sequential order and alternation of colour are retained. Worrying-back is allowed.

92

Fig. 71

When all the cards of a column have been played, the top card of the sealed packet immediately above the vacancy is turned face upwards and brought into play. It need not necessarily be used to fill the vacancy, which may be filled by any exposed card, or by a sequence.

The stock is dealt one card at a time, and any card that

Fig. 71 Fandango
The 4 ♥ is packed on the 5 ♥, the 7 ♠ on the 8 ♠, the 6 ♠ on the 7 ♠ and the 9 ♦ on the 10 ♦. The K ♥ is packed on the Q ♥ and the Q ♥ on the K ♥. And so on.

cannot be built on a foundation nor packed on the lay-out is played to a waste-heap, the top card of which is available to be played.

When the stock is exhausted, the waste-heap is taken in hand as a new stock. The three top cards are dealt face upwards on the table as a reserve. If any or all of them can be played, cards from the stock are dealt to bring the reserve up to three cards. Play continues in this way until either the game succeeds, or fails because no further play can be made and the reserve is full.

There is rarely any hurry to pack on the cards in the lay-out; it is more important to open up the sealed packets. Make the most out of worrying-back, moving sequences from one column to another and obtaining vacancies.

Fandango

Play to the board face upwards 60 cards in 20 fans of three cards each. If any Aces occur in the fans play them to the centre as foundation-cards and replace them in the fans with cards from the stock. As they become available, the other Aces are played to the centre (*see* Fig. 71).

The object of the game is to build ascending suit sequences on the Aces to the Kings.

The exposed cards of the fans are available to be built on the foundations, or they may be packed on each other in ascending or descending suit sequences which may be reversed at will. A vacancy in the lay-out, because all the cards of a fan have been played, is filled by a new fan of three cards from the stock.

Three deals are allowed. When no further moves can be made, the lay-out is picked up, shuffled together with any cards left in the stock, and redealt to the board in fans of three cards each. An Ace, but no other card, occurring in a fan may be played to the foundation-row and replaced by a card from the stock.

Fifty

Play the top card of the pack to the centre, in order to determine the foundations.

Deal the next 49 cards face downwards in a row of seven packets of seven cards each, and turn the top cards of the packets face upwards (*see* Fig. 72).

94

The object of the game is to release the remaining seven foundation-cards, play them to the centre, and build on them round-the-corner suit sequences.

The face-upwards cards on each packet are not packed on. They are available to be built on the foundations, or packed on the top card of the waste-heap in a descending, round-the-corner sequence of alternate colour.

When a card is played from a packet in the lay-out, the card under it is turned face upwards and is available to be played. A vacancy is filled either by the top card of the waste-heap or that of a packet.

The stock is turned three cards at a time to a single waste-heap. If at the end of a deal there are only two cards in the stock they are treated as three; if there is only one card, it is placed at the bottom of the waste-heap to become the bottom card of the first bundle of three in the redeal. The stock is dealt and redealt until either the game is won, or lost because no further play can be made.

Fig. 72 Fifty
As they become available, the other 10s are played to the foundation-row.
Round-the-corner suit sequences are built on the 10s to the 9s.
The J ♠ is built on the 10 ♠ and the card under it is exposed (K ♣).
The top card of the bundle of three from the stock is the 7 ♥ and on it are packed the 6 ♠ and 5 ♥ from the lay-out, exposing the cards under them.
And so on.

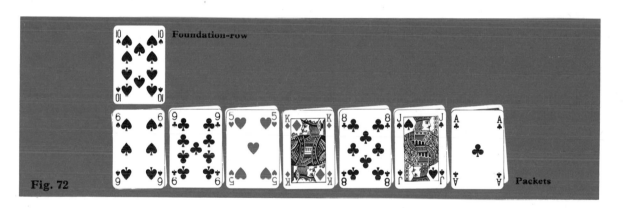

Fig. 72

Form Fours

Remove from the pack and play to the centre as foundation-cards a red Ace, King, Queen and Knave, and a black Ace, King, Queen and Knave. The suits are immaterial. The two colours should be arranged in two groups side by side (*see* Fig. 73).

The object of the game is to build ascending colour sequences on the Aces to Kings, and on the Queens, round-the-corner, to Knaves; and descending colour sequences on the Kings to Aces, and on the Knaves, round-the-corner, to Queens.

Eight cards are dealt face upwards in a row to the board, and any available cards are built on the foundations, or packed on each other one card at a time in ascending or descending sequences of alternate colour at the option of the player.

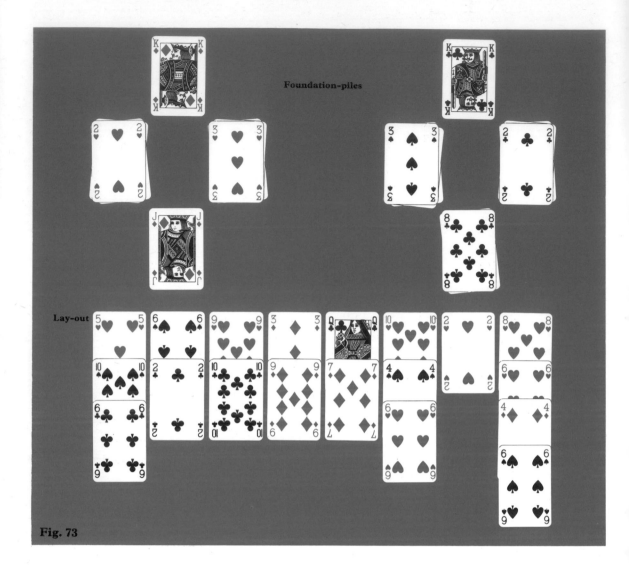

Fig. 73

Fig. 73 Form Fours

During the play the red Ace has been built up to a 2 and the Queen to a 3.

The black Ace has been built up to a 3, the Queen to a 2, and the Knave down to an 8.

The 9 ♦ is packed on the 10 ♣ and the 3 ♦ built on the 2 ♥.

The vacancy is filled with the 6 ♥, the 4 ♠ is built on the 3 ♠, and the 10 ♥ on the J ♦.

The 6 ♠ is packed on the 7 ♦.

And so on.

A vacancy in the lay-out may be filled either by an exposed card or by a sequence.

When all building and packing has been completed, another eight cards are dealt to the lay-out, covering those cards in position and filling any vacancies.

The game ends when the stock has been exhausted.

Four Square

Four Square is considered an easy game that the player will win every time unless he plays carelessly or is dogged by bad luck.

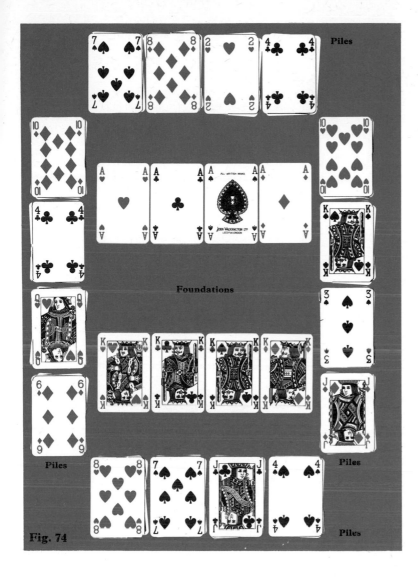

Fig. 74 Four Square
The 2 ♥ is built on the A ♥ and the Q ♥ on the K ♥.
The 3 ♠ is packed on the 4 ♠ (or the 4 ♠ on the 3 ♠) and the 10 ♦ on the J ♦ (or the J ♦ on the 10 ♦).
And so on.

Remove from the pack an Ace and a King of each suit and play them to the board as foundation-cards. Deal the remainder of the pack face downwards in 16 piles of six cards each, arrange them in a square with the foundation-cards in the middle, and turn the top cards of the piles face upwards (*see* Fig. 74).

The object of the game is to build ascending suit sequences on the Aces to the Kings, and descending suit sequences on the Kings to the Aces. When the top cards of two foundations of the same suit are in sequence, the cards of either may be reversed onto the other, except for the original Ace or King foundation-card.

The top cards of the piles are exposed and may be built on the foundations, or packed on each other either in ascending or descending suit sequences, which may be on the same pile.

Only one card may be moved at a time, and when a card is taken from a pile the card under it is turned face upwards and becomes available for play. A vacancy, when all the cards of a pile have been played, is not filled.

When all possible moves have been made and play comes to a standstill, the player has the grace of bringing the bottom cards of some or all of the piles to the top. Three such graces are allowed.

Half Moon

Deal to the board, as a reserve, eight cards face upwards in a row. Deal the rest of the pack face downwards in 12 packets of eight cards each. Arrange the packets in a semi-circle above the reserve, and turn face upwards the top card of each packet (*see* Fig. 75).

Fig. 75 Half Moon
The 6 ♠ is taken with the 5 ♥. The cards under the 3 ♥ and 3 ♦ are looked at to determine which is the better to take with the 8 ♥. The cards under the 7 ♣ and 7 ♠ are looked at to determine which is the better to take with the 4 ♠. The 9 ♥ is taken either with the 2 ♠ or 2 ♣, and the 10 ♦ with the A ♠.
And so on.

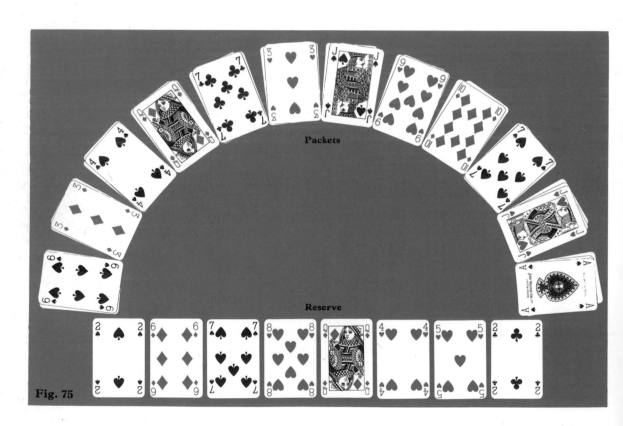

Fig. 75

The object of the game is to discard the pack by taking out of the game any two exposed cards whose pips total 11, and any sequences of King, Queen, Knave exposed together.

When the top card of a packet is taken, the card under it is

98

turned face upwards and becomes available for play. A card must not be taken from the reserve if one of the same rank can be taken from a packet; and if two or more cards of the same rank are available on top of the packets, the cards under them may be looked at to determine which one is the best to take.

Heads and Tails

Deal face upwards to the board a row of eight cards (the heads), then a row of eight packets each of 11 cards, then a row of eight cards (the tails) (*see* Fig. 76).

The object of the game is to release one Ace and one King of each suit, play then to the centre as foundation-cards, and build ascending suit sequences on the Aces to the Kings and descending suit sequences on the Kings to the Aces.

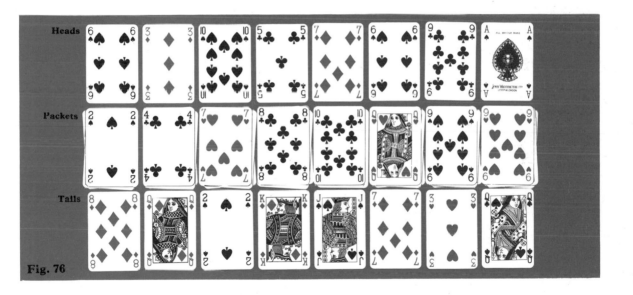

Fig. 76 Heads and Tails
The A ♠ is played to the centre and the 9 ♥ fills the vacancy.
The K ♦ is played to the centre, the Q ♦ is built on it and the 8 ♣ and 4 ♣ fill the vacancies.
The J ♠ is packed on the Q ♠, the 10 ♠ on the J ♠, and the vacancies filled by the 10 ♣ and 7 ♥.
And so on.

Only the cards in the top and bottom rows are available to be built on the foundations. They may also be packed in ascending and descending, round-the-corner suit sequences. The cards from the middle row of packets are used only to fill vacancies in the top and bottom rows. The card must be taken from the packet immediately above or below the vacancy, unless the packet has already been consumed, when a card may be taken from any packet.

Heap

Lay out as foundation-cards a sequence of 13 cards in alternate colour, from a 7 to a 6. The suits are immaterial. The rest of the pack is dealt face upwards to the board in 22 fans of four cards each and one of three cards (*see* Fig. 77).

The object of the game is to build on the 13 foundation-cards numeral-sequences of eight cards in the same colour on the first 12, and in alternate colour on the thirteenth. If the game is successful (and it should be with the exercise of forethought) it will show a sequence from Ace to Knave in alternate colour and the Queen and King of the same colour.

There is no packing on the lay-out, and no filling of a vacancy when all the cards of a fan have been played. The top cards of the fans are available to be built on the foundations, and, when every available card has been built on the foundations, those remaining in the lay-out are picked up, shuffled and redealt in fans of four each. Any over-cards (one, two or three) have a fan to themselves.

Only two deals are allowed.

Keep the sequences on the foundation-cards as equal as possible.

Nothing is to be gained by playing off all the cards of a fan, because the vacancy is not filled. Therefore, if two cards of the same rank are available at the same time, play the one from the fan with more cards in it.

Hypotenuse

The name is nothing to worry about, and there is no need to grab a dictionary. Those who have forgotten their geometry are reminded that the hypotenuse is that side of a triangle which is opposite a right angle.

An Ace and a King of each suit are removed from the pack and played to the centre as foundation-cards. Forty-five cards are dealt face upwards to the board in a row of nine cards, eight cards, seven cards, and so down to one card. The lay-out is unusual because the first card (that is the card at the extreme left of the first row) is placed vertically, but the second card is placed horizontally, and so vertically-horizontally-vertically to the single card at the bottom of the triangular lay-out which is placed vertically (*see* Fig. 78).

The object of the game is to build ascending suit sequences

Foundation-row

Lay-out

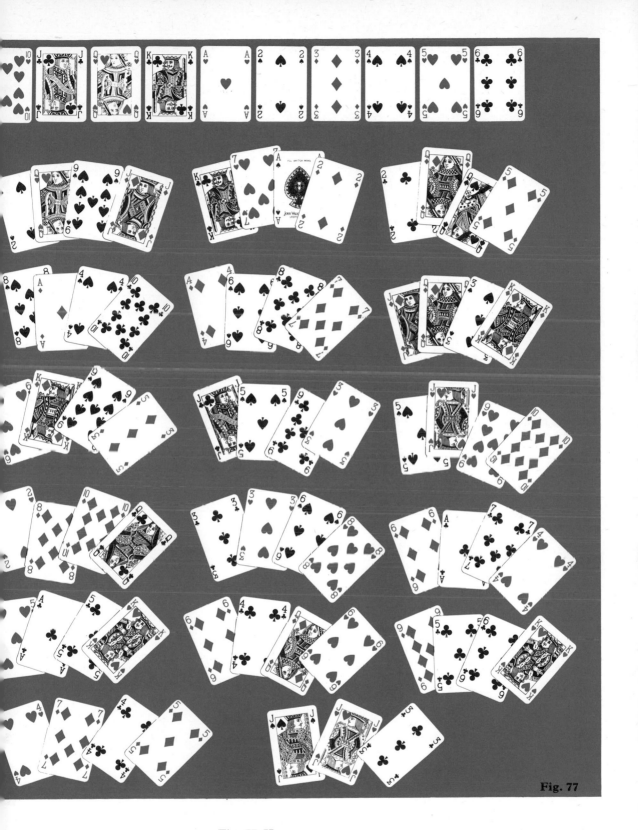

Fig. 77 Heap

The J ♦ is built on the 10 ♥, the 2 ♦ on the A ♥, the 10 ♣ on the 9 ♣, the J ♠ on the 10 ♣, the 7 ♦ on the 6 ♣ and the 8 ♠ on the 7 ♦.

And so on.

101

Fig. 78 Hypotenuse

The 2 ♦ is built on the A ♦,
and the Q ♥ on the K ♥.
The 8 ♠ is packed on the 9 ♣, the
7 ♣ on the 8 ♠, the 6 ♦ on the
7 ♣, the 5 ♣ on the 6 ♦ and the
4 ♥ on the 5 ♣.
This frees the 3 ♦ which is built
on the 2 ♦.
As no more moves are available, a
card is dealt from the stock to the
waste-heap.
And so on.

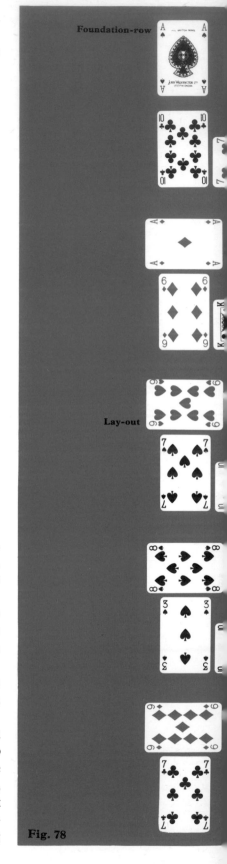

Foundation-row

Lay-out

Fig. 78

on the Aces to the Kings, and descending suit sequences on
the Kings to the Aces. When the top cards of two foundation-
piles of the same suit are in sequence, any or all of the cards
of one pile (except for the original Ace- or King-foundation)
may be reversed onto the other.

In the lay-out the exposed cards are those on the hypotenuse, and then only when they are free on one side and
also at either top or bottom. Cards that are free may be built
on a foundation or packed in a descending sequence, regardless of suit and colour, on the top card of the waste-heap.
There is no packing on cards in the lay-out, and, of course,
vacancies in the lay-out are not filled.

One redeal is allowed. Allah be praised.

Indian Carpet

Indian Carpet has a number of other names – Japanese Rug,
Quilt and Crazy Quilt – which speak for its popularity. It is,
perhaps, no wonder because the lay-out is an attractive one
and the game easy to play.

Remove an Ace and a King of each suit and play them to
the centre as foundation-cards. Below them deal 64 cards
face upwards in eight rows of eight cards each, placing the
cards vertically and horizontally by turn (*see* Fig. 79).

The object of the game is to build ascending suit sequences
on the Aces to the Kings and descending suit sequences on
the Kings to the Aces.

There is no packing on the cards in the lay-out. The stock
is turned one card at a time, which is played to a waste-heap
if it cannot be built on a foundation. The top card of the
waste-heap is always available to be built on a foundation,
and it may be packed with the exposed cards of the lay-out
in ascending or descending, round-the-corner suit sequences. The exposed cards in the lay-out are those along

Waste-heap

103

Lay-out

Fig. 79

Waste-heap

104

Fig. 79 Indian Carpet
The 8 ♣ is packed on the 9 ♣ and the 2 ♥ built on the A ♥.

The 7 ♣ is freed to be packed on the 8 ♣ and the 6 ♣ is packed on the 7 ♣, freeing the Q ♥ to be built on the K ♥.

And so on.

the four sides of the square that have either the top or bottom (not the side) free. A card may not be isolated by removing those surrounding it.

The stock may be dealt twice.

The removal of a card from the lay-out releases one or more other cards. Look to see if two duplicate cards are buried in the lay-out. If they are, play should be directed to releasing one of them as soon as possible.

Fig. 80 Kings' Way
The 9 ♠ is packed on the 10 ♦ and the player has the option of packing either the 10 ♥ or the 8 ♥ on the 9 ♠.

He will be best advised to choose the 8 ♥, because when he faces the cards under the 9 ♠ and 8 ♥, one of them may be a black 7 which can then be packed on the 8 ♥ and followed by the 6 ♦.

And so on.

Kings' Way

To the best of my knowledge Kings' Way is unlike any other game of patience. For this reason, and no other, it is included in this collection. Except for originality it is a game with few merits and it gives no scope for skill or ingenuity. Success depends entirely on the fortuitous order of the cards.

Remove the eight Kings from the pack and play them in a row face upwards to the top of the board. Below them deal 40 cards in five overlapping rows of eight cards each, the

Fig. 80

first four rows face downwards, the fifth face upwards (*see* Fig. 80).

The object of the game is to clear the 40 cards (not to include the Kings) dealt to the board, so that the road is open to the Kings – the way to the Kings, the Kings' Way.

There is no building on foundations and no packing on cards in the lay-out. The stock is dealt one card at a time to a waste-heap and the eight cards in the bottom row of the lay-out are exposed and may be packed on the top card of the waste-heap either in ascending or descending sequence of alternate colour. When a card from the bottom row of the lay-out is packed on the waste-heap, the card in the row above it is turned face upwards and becomes available.

Aces are given special treatment. If one is turned up in the lay-out it can only be moved when a 2 of an alternate colour is the top card of the waste-heap. If one is dealt from the stock to the waste-heap it may be packed with a 2 of an alternate colour if one is exposed in the lay-out, as also may subsequent cards in sequence. If no 2 of alternate colour is exposed in the lay-out, the Ace is moved to a separate waste-heap, as also are any others that are dealt when no 2 is available. They remain there until the stock is exhausted and, if the game has not already been won, the number of Aces in the waste-heap determines the number of cards that may be taken from the beginning of the waste-heap and dealt a second time.

An easy game that does not tax the intelligence; it is quite an amusing one.

Lady Palk

Whoever she was or is, I do not know, but she has certainly given her name to an interesting patience.

Deal face upwards to the board 16 cards in four columns of four cards each. This is the left wing. Then, leaving a space wide enough to accommodate the eight Aces in two columns of four cards each, deal another 16 cards in four columns of four cards each. This is the right wing (*see* Fig. 81).

The object of the game is to release the eight Aces, play them to the centre as foundation-cards, and build on them ascending suit sequences to the Kings.

The cards in the left-hand column of the left wing, and those in the right-hand column of the right wing, are exposed. They may be built on the foundations, packed on other exposed cards in the lay-out or be themselves packed on, in descending sequences irrespective of suit and colour. A card, and a sequence either in part or as a whole, may be moved from an exposed card to any other, provided the sequential order is retained.

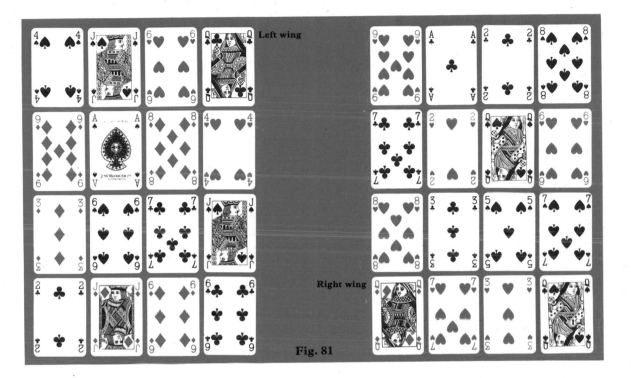

Left wing

Right wing

Fig. 81

The stock is dealt one card at a time, and any card that cannot be built on a foundation nor packed on the lay-out is played to a waste-heap, the top card of which is available for play.

If all the cards of a row are moved, the vacancy may be filled only by a King.

The stock is dealt only once, but worrying back is allowed throughout the game.

Fig. 81 Lady Palk
The 3 ♦ is packed on the 4 ♠ and the 2 ♣ on the 3 ♦.
The 8 ♠ is packed on the 9 ♦, the 7 ♠ on the 8 ♠, the 6 ♥ on the 7 ♠ and the 5 ♠ on the 6 ♥.
The 2 ♣ is packed on the 3 ♣, the A ♣ is played to the centre, and the 2 ♣ and 3 ♣ are built on the A ♣.
And so on.

Le Cadran

Le Cadran is described by Lady Adelaide Cadogan in her *Illustrated Games of Patience* of *circa* 1870. It is, therefore, one of the oldest, if not the oldest, of the many building-up patience games.

Deal 40 cards face upwards to the board in four overlapping rows of 10 cards each (*see* Fig. 82).

107

The object of the game is to release the eight Aces, play them to the centre as foundation-cards, and build ascending suit sequences on them to the Kings.

The bottom cards of the columns are available to be played to the foundations, packed on exposed cards in the lay-out, or themselves be packed on, in descending suit sequences. Cards must be moved only singly, not in sequences.

Fig. 82

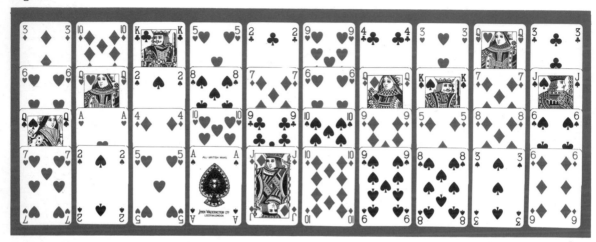

Fig. 82 *Le Cadran*
Play the A ♠ to the centre, build the 2 ♠ on the A ♠ and the 3 ♠ on the 2 ♠.
Play the A ♥ to the centre.
Pack the 10 ♦ on the J ♦, the 9 ♠ on the 10 ♠, the 9 ♦ on the 10 ♦, the 8 ♦ on the 9 ♦, the 7 ♦ on the 8 ♦ and the 6 ♦ on the 7 ♦.
And so on.

A vacancy, when all the cards of a column have been played, is filled either with an exposed card from the lay-out or with the top card of the waste-heap.

The stock is dealt one card at a time, and any card that cannot be built on a foundation nor packed on the lay-out, is played to a waste-heap, the top card of which is always available.

There is no second deal.

Le Château

Deal 60 cards face upwards to the board in 12 packets of five cards each, in a row of three packets, then of four packets and of five packets, touching each other only at the corners (*see* Fig. 83).

The object of the game is to release the Aces, play them to the centre as foundation-cards and build them up in suit sequences to the Kings.

The top card of a packet is exposed and may be built on a foundation or packed on the top card of another packet, or may itself be packed on, in a descending sequence of alter-

108

nate colour. A sequence may be moved from one packet to another either as a whole or in part, so long as the sequence and alternation of colour are retained.

The stock is turned one card at a time, and any card that cannot be played to a foundation nor to a packet is played to a waste-heap, the top card of which is always available for play.

A vacancy, caused by all the cards of a packet having been

Fig. 83 *Le Château*
The A ♠ is played to the centre, the 2 ♥ is packed on the 3 ♠, the 9 ♣ on the 10 ♥ and the 6 ♥ on the 7 ♣.
And so on.

Fig. 83

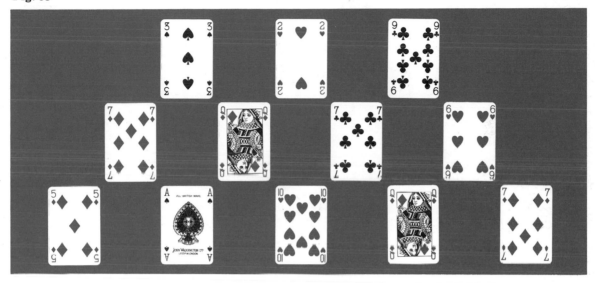

played, may be filled with the top card of the waste-heap, or by a card, sequence or part-sequence from one of the packets.

Les Huits

Les Huits is a building-up patience that offers scope for judgement. A glance at the illustration (Fig. 84) suggests that it is complicated, but the illustration is deceptive and the game by no means as difficult as it appears on the surface.

Deal face upwards to the board 64 cards in eight overlapping rows of eight cards each.

The object of the game is to release the eight Aces, play them to the centre as foundation-cards, and build on them ascending suit sequences to the Kings.

The bottom cards of the columns are available to be built on the foundations, or packed on each other in descending sequences regardless of suit and colour. A sequence or part of one may be moved from the foot of one column to that of

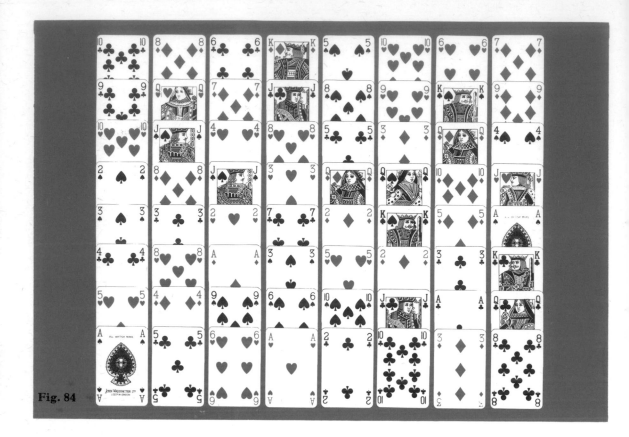

Fig. 84

Fig. 84 *Les Huits*

The A ♠ and A ♥ are played to
the centre.

The 5 ♣ is packed on the 6 ♥ and
the 5 ♥ on the 6 ♠.

The 4 ♣ is packed on the 5 ♣ and
the 3 ♦ on the 4 ♣.

The A ♣ is played to the centre.

The 2 ♣ is built on the A ♣ and
the 3 ♣ on the 2 ♣.

And so on.

another, provided, of course, the sequential order is retained. A vacancy, when all the cards of a column have been
played, is filled either with an exposed card or with a suit
sequence.

The stock is dealt one card at a time and any card that
cannot be built on a foundation nor packed on the lay-out
is played to the foot of the left-hand column.

The game ends when the stock is exhausted.

Matrimony

This is rather a difficult game but it has the merit of an
unusual lay-out and play.

Remove from the pack one Queen and one Knave of
Diamonds and play them to the centre as foundation-cards.
As they become available, play to the centre the two Knaves
of Hearts and the four black 10s. Below the foundation-row,
deal, face upwards, 16 cards in two rows of eight cards each
(*see* Fig. 85); foundation-cards are played directly to the
centre.

The object of the game is to build an ascending suit

110

sequence on the Queen of Diamonds to the Knave, and descending suit sequences on the three Knaves to the Queens, and on the four 10s to the Knaves. In all cases, of course, the sequences are round-the-corner, the Ace being above the King and below the 2.

The cards in the lay-out are exposed and available to be

Fig. 85

built on the foundations. When all plays have been made, 16 cards are dealt from the stock to the lay-out, covering the cards that have not been played from it and filling the vacancies left by those that have. Play is continued in this way until the stock is exhausted.

When play comes to a standstill and the stock exhausted, each pile in turn (beginning with the one at the extreme right of the lower row) is picked up and dealt from left to right as far as it will go, the first card being dealt to the vacancy made where the pile was taken up. The game ends, if it has not been won before, after the pile at the extreme left of the upper row has been dealt.

Fig. 85 Matrimony
The J ♥ and 10 ♠ were played to the foundation-row during the deal.
The K ♦ is built on the Q ♦ and the 9 ♠ on the 10 ♠.
No further plays are available, so 16 cards are dealt from the stock covering the unplayed cards and filling the two vacancies.
And so on.

Miss Milligan

Whoever the lady is or was she has given her name to one of the best of the double-pack patiences, that demands ingenuity if it is to be successful.

Deal the cards face upwards to the board in overlapping rows of eight cards each. Until all eight cards have been dealt no play may be made, but after dealing the eight cards,

111

make what plays you can before dealing the next row (*see* Fig. 86).

The object of the game is to play the eight Aces to the

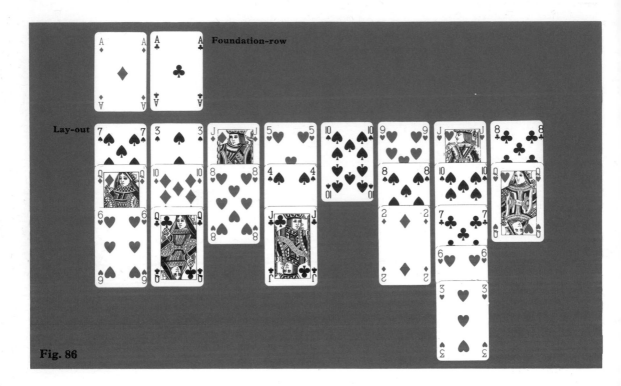

Fig. 86

Fig. 86 Miss Milligan
The J ♣ is packed on the Q ♥ , the 3 ♥ on the 4 ♠ and the 7 ♣ with the 6 ♥ on the 8 ♥ .
The 2 ♦ is built on the A ♦ , the J ♥ with the 10 ♠ is packed on the Q ♣ and the 9 ♥ with the 8 ♠ on either 10 ♠ .
And so on.

centre as foundation-cards, to be built on in ascending suit sequences to the Kings.

In the lay-out the bottom cards of the eight columns are exposed. They may be built on a foundation, packed on other exposed cards in the lay-out or themselves be packed on, in descending sequences of alternate colour. A sequence may be moved from one column to another only as a whole, and, of course, only so long as the sequential order and alternation of colour are retained. A vacancy may be filled only by a King or a sequence headed by a King; if left vacant, the column will be filled when the next row of eight cards is dealt.

When the stock is exhausted, waiving is allowed. If an exposed card is blocking the run of a sequence it may be lifted and held in hand until further plays enable the player to return it to the lay-out. Waiving may be repeated as often as the player chooses, but only one card at a time may be waived.

112

Mount Olympus

Remove the Aces and 2s from the pack and play them to the centre in two rows (the Aces above the 2s) as foundation-cards. Below them deal, face upwards, a row of nine cards (*see* Fig. 87).

The object of the game is to build suit sequences on the Aces in the order A.3.5.7.9.J.K. and on the 2s in the order 2.4.6.8.10.Q.

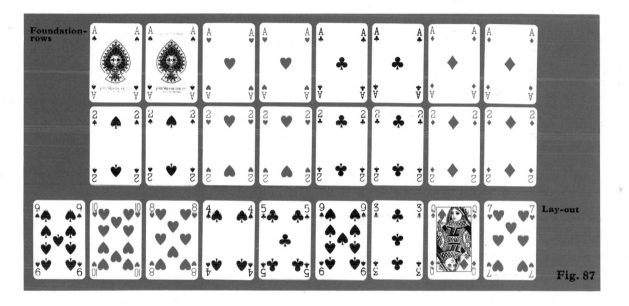

Fig. 87

The cards in the lay-out are available to be built on the foundations, or packed on each other, in descending suit sequences by twos. A sequence may be moved only as a whole, and a vacancy, caused by moving a card or sequence, must be filled from the stock.

When play comes to a standstill, all vacancies must be filled and, if no further moves can be made, a row of nine cards is dealt on top of those in the lay-out. The top cards of the piles in the lay-out are exposed and available for play.

Fig. 87 Mount Olympus
The 8 ♥ is packed on the 10 ♥.
The 3 ♣ is built on an A ♣ and the 5 ♣ on the 3 ♣.
The vacancies are filled by cards from the stock and, if none can be built on the foundations nor packed on exposed cards in the lay-out, a row of cards is dealt on top of those in the lay-out.
And so on.

Mrs Mop

Mrs Mop, a patience invented by the late Mr Charles Jewell, is rather a deceptive game. It appears to be one that is easy

113

Fig. 88

to play, but, in fact, is not. Success comes only if thought is given to every move, sometimes right up to the end of the game.

The name is an appropriate one, because if the player is to succeed he must clear, or mop up, a column early in the game, in order to gain a vacancy to transfer cards from one column to another. Without one the chance of success is remote.

Deal face upwards to the board the whole pack in eight overlapping rows of 13 cards each (*see* Fig. 88).

There are no foundation-cards. The object of the game is to build within the lay-out eight descending suit sequences on the Kings to the Aces.

The cards at the foot of the columns may be packed on each other in descending sequences regardless of suit and colour. Only one card may be moved at a time, unless two or more cards are in suit sequence when they must all be moved together.

When all the cards of a column have been moved, the vacancy may be filled either by a single card or by a suit sequence of cards.

Fig. 88 Mrs Mop

The J ♣ is packed on the Q ♣, the 9 ♠ on the 10 ♠, the 2 ♣ on the 3 ♣ and the A ♠ on the 2 ♠. The 5 ♥ is packed on the 6 ♥, the Q ♣ with the J ♣ on the K ♣ and the 3 ♦ on the 4 ♦. The 2 ♠ with the A ♠ is packed on the 3 ♦, and the 3 ♣ with the 2 ♣ on the 4 ♣. And so on.

114

Fig. 89

Fig. 89 Napoleon's Square
The A ♥ is played to the centre,
the 5 ♠ is packed on the 6 ♠ and
the 3 ♦ on the 4 ♦.
Either Q ♣ may be packed on the
K ♣ and the cards in the piles
should first be looked at to
determine the more favourable
play.
And so on.

Napoleon's Square

Deal face upwards to the board 48 cards in 12 piles of four
cards each, arranged as three sides of a square (*see* Fig. 89).

The object of the game is to play the eight Aces, as they
become available, to the centre of the square as foundations,
on which to build ascending suit sequences to the Kings.

The top cards of the piles are exposed. They may be
built on the foundations, packed on other exposed cards or
themselves be packed on, in descending suit sequences. All
cards in sequence at the top of a pile may be lifted as a whole
and played elsewhere, and the vacancy, when all the cards
of a pile have been moved, may be filled by a card or sequence from the top of another pile, by a card from the stock
or by the top card of the waste-heap.

The stock is dealt one card at a time and any card that
cannot be built on a foundation nor packed on the lay-out
is played to a waste-heap, the top card of which is always
available to be played.

The stock may be dealt only once.

The player is permitted to look at all the cards in a pile.

115

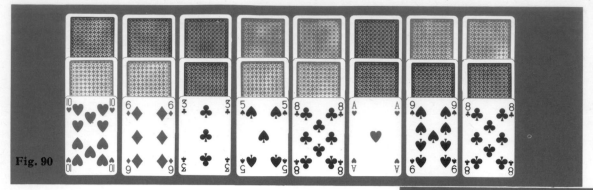

Fig. 90

Octave

Deal to the board 24 cards in three overlapping rows of eight cards each, the first and second rows face downwards, the third face upwards (*see* Fig. 90).

The object of the game is to release the Aces, play them to the centre as foundation-cards and build on them ascending suit sequences to the 10s, and following above them a row of Knaves, another of Queens and a third of Kings.

The face-upwards cards in the bottom row of the lay-out are available to be built on the foundations, and may be packed in descending sequences of alternate colour. Cards and sequences, either wholly or in part, may be moved from one exposed card in the lay-out to another, provided the sequential order and alternation of colour are retained.

When a card is moved from the bottom row of the lay-out, the face-downwards card immediately above it is turned face upwards and becomes available to be played. A vacancy, when all the cards of a column have been played, may be filled by any exposed card or sequence of cards.

The stock is turned one card at a time, and any card that cannot be built on a foundation nor packed on the lay-out is played to a waste-heap, the top card of which is always available to be played.

When the stock is exhausted, the waste-heap is turned and the top eight cards are taken in hand as a reserve. These cards may be used for building on the foundations or packing on the lay-out, and any further plays from the lay-out may be made. When a card is played from the reserve another is taken from the top of the waste-heap to bring the total number of cards in the reserve to eight. There is no redeal, and the game ends when the reserve is full and no further play can be made.

Fig. 91

Fig. 90 Octave

The A ♥ is played to the centre.
The 5 ♠ is packed on the 6 ♦ and
the 9 ♠ on the 10 ♥
The face-downwards cards
released by playing the A ♥, 5 ♠
and 9 ♠ are turned face upwards.
And so on.

Fig. 91 Paganini

The eight Aces are removed and
the player must decide which rows
he will allot to the suits.
Obviously he will allot the first
row to Clubs, because the 4 ♣ and
5 ♣ are already in position.
An A ♣, therefore, is placed to the
left of the 6 ♥
The second row is allotted to
Hearts because the 7 ♥ is in
position and the 5 ♥ is quite well
placed.
An A ♥, therefore, is placed to the
left of the 9 ♦
And so on.

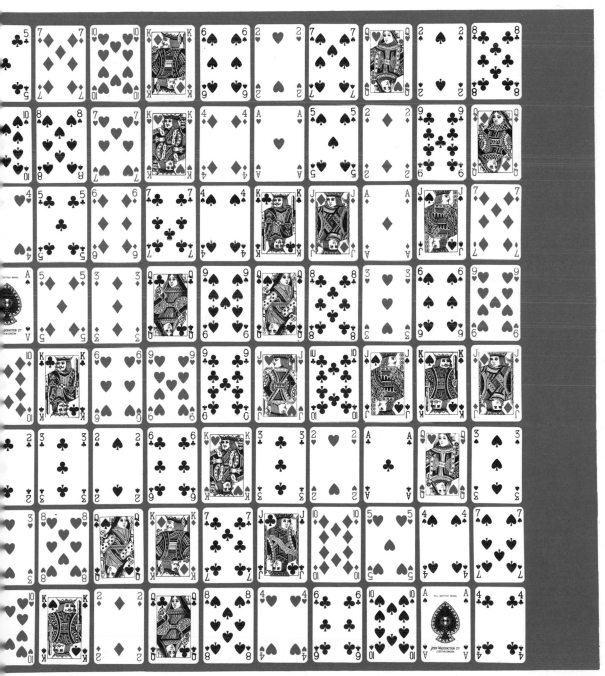

117

Paganini

Paganini, devised by the late Mr Charles Jewell, is a variation of the single-pack game of Vacancies (p. 61). The fact that it is played with 104 cards, instead of only 52, makes it considerably more difficult, and at the start the player is faced with the problem of having to decide which rows he will allot to the suits. You have been warned!

The whole pack is dealt face upwards to the board in eight rows of 13 cards each (*see* Fig. 91).

The object of the game is to allot a suit to each row, place the Ace at the extreme left of the row, and arrange the cards so that each row consists of one suit in sequence, beginning with the Ace and ending with the King.

The play consists in filling a vacancy in the lay-out with the next higher card of the same suit as the card on the left of the vacancy. When a vacancy is filled it leaves another in the lay-out, and the play continues until a run is stopped by removing a card from the right-hand side of a King, because no card may be played to the right of a King.

Only one deal is allowed. Those who wish an easier game, however, may allow themselves one or two redeals. When a deal is brought to an end, the cards in the lay-out that are out of sequence are picked up, shuffled, and the lay-out remade by dealing the cards to the board with a vacancy in each row to the immediate right of the cards that are in sequence.

Ace-founda

Fig. 92

Parallels

Remove from the pack an Ace and a King of each suit. Play the Aces in a column to the left of the board, and the Kings in a column to the right. Between the two columns deal face upwards a row of 10 cards (*see* Fig. 92).

The object of the game is to build ascending suit sequences on the Aces to the Kings, and descending suit sequences on the Kings to the Aces.

The cards in the row are available to be built on the foundations. The vacancies are filled from the stock. When play comes to a halt, a second row of 10 cards is dealt below the first. The deal continues in this way until the stock is exhausted. The play is governed by the following rules:

1. The only cards that are available to be built on the

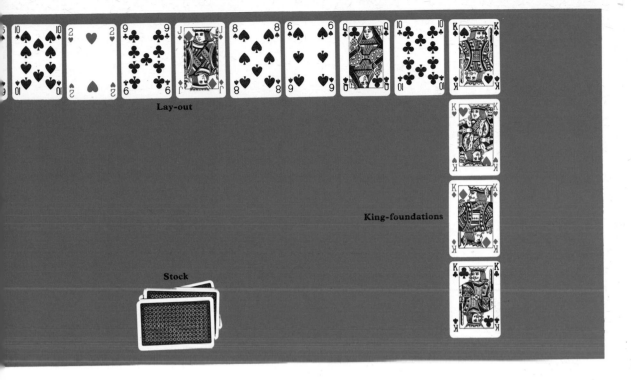

Lay-out

King-foundations

Stock

foundations are those from the rows and which have one of their shorter sides free.

2. Cards must not be built on a foundation until all 10 cards of a row have been dealt.

3. When any vacancy is filled, all vacancies must be filled.

4. A row of 10 cards may not be dealt until all vacancies have been filled.

5. Vacancies must be filled from left to right and from top to bottom.

6. There is no compulsion to build a card on a foundation.

7. When the two top foundation-cards of the same suit are in sequence, either may be reversed onto the other, with the exception of the Ace or King at the bottom.

8. It is not permissible (even in this permissive age) to look at the top card of the stock before deciding on a play.

Fig. 92 Parallels
The 2 ♥ is built on the A ♥, the Q ♣ on the K ♣, and the vacancies filled from the stock. And so on.

Parisian

Play an Ace and a King of each suit to the centre. Below them deal face upwards to the board four cards, and put aside two cards face downwards (*see* Fig. 93).

The object of the game is to build ascending suit sequences on the Aces to the Kings, and descending suit sequences on the Kings to the Aces.

119

The exposed cards in the lay-out are available to be built on the foundations. When no further play can be made, four cards are dealt from the stock to cover those cards in position and fill any vacancies, and two cards are put aside face downwards. Dealing is continued in this way until the stock is exhausted. When it is, the face-downwards cards are turned face upwards, and further plays, if any, are made with them and with the cards in the lay-out.

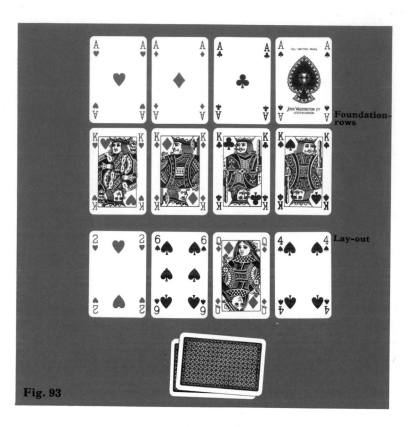

Fig. 93 Parisian
The 2 ♥ is built on the A ♥ and the Q ♦ on the K ♦.
As no more plays are to be made, four cards are dealt from the stock to fill the vacancies left by the 2 ♥ and Q ♦, and to cover the 6 ♠ and 4 ♠.
Two more cards are dealt face downwards.
And so on.

Fig. 93

Foundation-rows

Lay-out

Four deals in all are allowed. To form a new stock, the piles in the lay-out are picked up and shuffled and the un-played cards of the reserve are placed at the bottom of the pack. The redeals are made in the same way as the first deal, except that in the fourth, and final, deal all the cards are dealt face upwards to the lay-out, and no cards are put aside face downwards.

Patriarchs

Remove from the pack one Ace and one King of each suit, and play them to the board in two columns, the Aces to the left and the Kings to the right. In between deal face upwards nine cards in three rows of three cards each (*see* Fig. 94).

The object of the game is to build ascending suit sequences on the Aces to the Kings, and descending suit sequences on the Kings to the Aces. When the top cards of the two foundations of the same suit are in sequence, any or all of the cards (except the original foundation-cards) may be reversed onto the other.

All the cards in the lay-out are available to be built on the

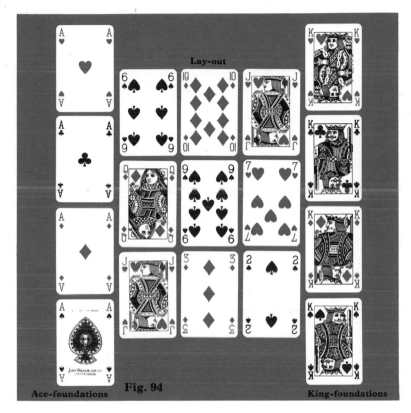

Fig. 94 **Patriarchs**
The Q ♦ may be built on the K ♦ and the 2 ♠ on the A ♠.
As yet there is no waste-heap, and the vacancies, therefore, are filled from the stock.
And so on.

foundations, and the vacancies by so doing must be filled at once from the waste-heap, or from the stock if there is no waste-heap.

The stock is dealt one card at a time, and the card played to a waste-heap if it cannot be built on a foundation. The top card of the waste-heap is available to be built on a foundation. A redeal, but only one, is allowed.

Pendant

Pendant gets its name because the first 18 cards of the pack are arranged face upwards on the board in the form of a pendant: 12 cards are placed in pairs, close together, side by

121

side, and then half-covered by six cards placed over them. A column of six cards is dealt face upwards on both sides of the pendant, and the next card of the pack is played to the centre as the first foundation-card (*see* Fig. 95).

The object of the game is to release the other seven foundation-cards, play them to the centre, and build on them round-the-corner suit sequences of 13 cards each.

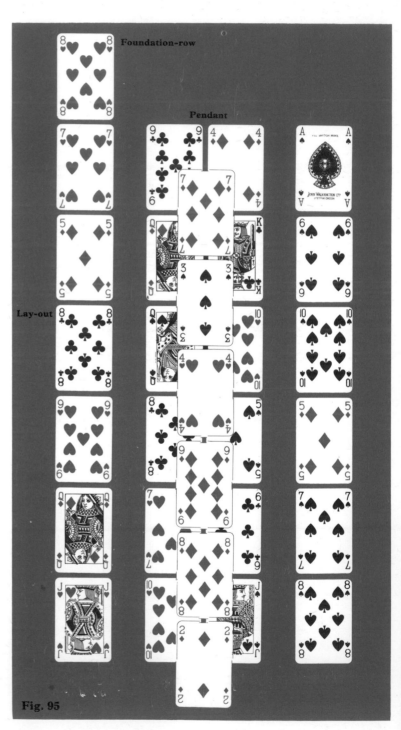

Fig. 95 Pendant
The 8 ♣ and 8 ♠ are played to the foundation-row.
The 9 ♥ is built on the 8 ♥.
Between each move the vacancies in the columns are filled.
The vacancy left by the 8 ♣ and 9 ♥ must be filled from the stock; the vacancy left by the 8 ♠ may be filled either from the stock or by the 2 ♦.
Obviously the 2 ♦ is better because it releases the 8 ♦ which is played to the foundation-row.
The 10 ♥ and J ♠ are released.
The 10 ♥ is built on the 9 ♥, the J ♥ on the 10 ♥ and the vacancy left by the J ♥ filled by the J ♠.
And so on.

There is no packing on the lay-out. The cards in the columns and the bottom card, or cards, of the pendant are available to be built on the foundations. A vacancy in the pendant is not filled: a vacancy in a column must be, however, before a further play is made. If the top or bottom card of a column has been played, the vacancy may be filled either with a card from the stock or one from the bottom of the pendant; if any other card in a column has been played the vacancy must be filled from the stock.

The stock is dealt one card at a time, and a card that cannot be built on a foundation, nor is needed to fill a vacancy in a column, is played to a waste-heap. When the stock is exhausted, the waste-heap is picked up and redealt. Redealing continues until the game is either won or lost.

Fig. 96 Persian
The J ♦ is packed on the Q ♠ and the A ♥ played to the foundation-row.
The 8 ♣ is packed on the 9 ♥, the 7 ♥ on the 8 ♣, the J ♠ on the Q ♦, the 8 ♥ on the 9 ♠ and the A ♠ is played to the foundation-row.
And so on.

Persian

Persian patience has the alternative name of Bezique patience. Why is not very clear. It could be because it is played with the 2s, 3s, 4s, 5s and 6s removed from the pack, as in

Fig. 96

123

bezique, but then they also are in piquet and such a pack is more usually known as the short or piquet pack.

The 64 cards in the pack, after the low cards have been removed, are dealt, face upwards, to the board in eight overlapping rows of eight cards each (*see* Fig. 96).

The object of the game is to release the Aces, play them to the centre as foundations and build on them ascending suit sequences (the 7 follows the Ace) to the Kings.

The bottom cards of the columns are exposed. They may be built on the foundations, packed on other exposed cards in the lay-out or be themselves packed on, in descending sequences of alternate colour. A sequence may be moved only as a whole. A vacancy in the lay-out may be filled with any exposed card or sequence.

Three deals are allowed. After a deal the remaining cards in the lay-out are picked up and shuffled before dealing them again in eight columns, which may now have less than eight cards in each. If no cards can be taken after the first deal it is not counted as one of the permitted three.

Plait

Deal face upwards to the board 20 cards arranged in the form of a plait; that is, the first card is placed diagonally to the right, the second half covering it and diagonally to the left, the third half covering it and diagonally to the right, and thus to the twentieth card. On each side of the plait deal face upwards a column of six cards. The next card of the pack is dealt to the centre to determine the foundation-cards (*see* Fig. 97).

As they become available the other seven cards of the same rank are played to the foundation-row, to be built on in ascending, round-the-corner suit sequences of 13 cards each.

The bottom card of the plait and the exposed cards in the columns are available to be built on the foundations. The exposed cards in the columns are packed on in descending suit sequences. A card played from the plait to a foundation or to a card in one of the columns is not replaced, but a card played from a column is. If the top or bottom card of a column is played, the player has the option of filling the vacancy either with the bottom card of the plait or the top card of the stock or that of the waste-heap. If any other of the cards in the column are played the vacancy must be filled either with the top card of the stock or that of the waste-heap. Only one card may be moved at a time; cards must not be moved in sequences.

124

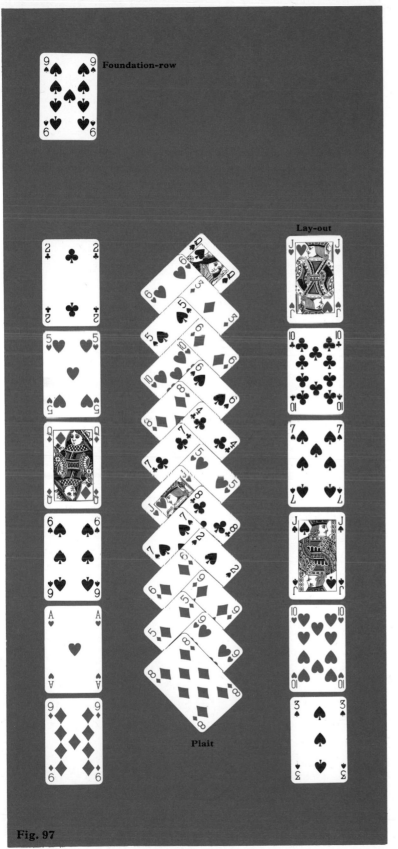

Fig. 97

Fig. 97 Plait

The 9 ♦ is played to the foundation-row and the vacancy is filled with the 8 ♦.

The 9 ♥ is played to the foundation-row, the 10 ♥ is built on the 9 ♥ and the J ♥ on the 10 ♥.

The vacancy left by the J ♥ is filled with the 5 ♦, and the 9 ♦ is played to the foundation-row.

The vacancy left by the 10 ♥ is filled from the stock.

The 6 ♠ is packed on the 7 ♠ and the vacancy filled from the stock. And so on.

125

The stock is dealt one card at a time, and any card that cannot be built on a foundation nor packed on the lay-out is played to a waste-heap, the top card of which is always available for play.

When the stock is exhausted, the waste-heap is picked up and redealt. Redealing continues until the game is either won or lost.

The game is a difficult one but interesting to play. Success depends very largely on making the best use of the cards in the plait.

Reversi

Reversi is a simple building-up patience with the unusual feature that the foundation-cards are built on in descending sequence, and the exposed cards in the lay-out packed in ascending sequence. The Ace is the lowest card of a suit.

The eight Kings are removed from the pack and arranged

Foundations

Fig. 98 Reversi
The 9 ♥ is packed on the 8 ♥, and the 5 ♦ on the 4 ♦.
The Q ♣ is built on the K ♣.
The vacancies are filled.
And so on.

Lay-out **Fig. 98** Lay-out

on the board in two rows each of four cards. Ten cards are dealt face upwards to the board in two columns each of five cards, one on each side of the foundation-cards (*see* Fig. 98).

The object of the game is to build descending suit sequences on the Kings to the Aces.

The cards in the lay-out are packed in ascending suit sequences, and, providing the sequential order is retained, a sequence, either as a whole or in part, may be moved from one exposed card to another. A vacancy must be filled either with a card from the stock or with the top card of the waste-heap. It must not be filled by any other card.

The stock is dealt one card at a time, and any card that is not played to a foundation nor to the lay-out is played to a single waste-heap, the top card of which is available for play. There is no second deal.

Robin Post

Robin Post is a new game invented by Colonel G. H. Latham, R.E. It is unquestionably one of the best, if not the best, of the double-pack patiences. Its one defect, if defect it is, is that the lay-out demands a very large table, even when small-sized cards are used.

Fifty-two cards are dealt face upwards to the board in a row of four, five, six, seven and eight cards; then seven, six, five and four cards. Between each card in the rows there should be a space of one card's width, so that the cards touch those in the row above them and below them only at the corners (*see* Fig. 99).

The object of the game is to release one Ace and one King of each suit, play them to the centre as foundations, and build ascending suit sequences on the Aces to the Kings, and descending suit sequences on the Kings to the Aces. If at any stage of the play the top cards of two foundations are in sequence, any or all of the cards (except the original Ace or King foundation-card) may be reversed onto the other.

The play is governed by six rules:

1. A card that has two or more corners free may be lifted and played.

2. A card that has only one corner free may not be lifted and played, but may be packed on in ascending or descending sequence of alternate colour. A sequence, once begun, may not be reversed.

3. A card that has no corner free may neither be lifted and played nor packed on.

4. A sequence in the lay-out may be moved from one card to another only as a whole and provided that the sequential order and alternation of colour is retained.

Fig. 99 Robin Post

At the start only the 9♥, 6♠, 8♦ and 3♥ in the top row, the 10♣ and 7♠ at each end of the middle row, and the 3♦, J♦, Q♠ and 7♠ in the bottom row may be lifted and played.

When, however, the 7♠ is lifted and packed either on the 8♦, 8♥ or 6♦, the A♠ may be lifted and played to the foundation-row, followed by the K♦.

More moves are now available since the 9♣ is freed to be packed either on the 8♦ or 8♥, and the

Fig. 99

128

9 ♥ is freed to be packed either on the 10 ♣ or 8 ♣, freeing the 2 ♦ that may be packed on the 3 ♣. And so on.

5. A sequence in the lay-out may be moved only onto a single card, and not onto another sequence.

6. At any stage of the game the player may refill the lay-out by dealing cards from the stock. The cards must be dealt from the original top row of the lay-out, from left to right, and, provided there are sufficient cards left in the stock, the lay-out must be completed before any further moves are made either to the foundations or within the lay-out.

Considerable thought has to be given to the play because a number of moves are always available—sometimes a large number—and every move that is made opens up the road to more.

Roosevelt's Favourite

The game is usually known as Spider, a name which I have rejected because a number of variations are known by the same name; in fact, Spider is not so much the name of any one game but the generic name for any game of patience in which the foundation-cards are not played to the centre, but in which sequences are built within the lay-out itself. I have suggested the alternative name of Roosevelt's Favourite because it is mentioned in the *Redbook Magazine* as being the favourite patience game of Franklin D. Roosevelt.

Deal to the board 40 cards in four overlapping rows of 10 cards each, the first, second and third rows face downwards, the fourth face upwards (see Fig. 100).

The object of the game is to build within the lay-out descending suit sequences on the Kings to the Aces. When a sequence has been completed it is removed from the lay-out, so that a successful game consists of clearing the board of all the cards in the pack.

The face-upwards cards at the bottom of the columns are packed in descending sequences regardless of suit, and sequences may be moved from one exposed card to another only as a whole. When a card or a sequence is moved from the bottom of a column, the face-downwards card immediately above it is turned face upwards and is available for play. When all the cards of a column have been moved and when a completed sequence is removed from the lay-out, the vacancy may be filled by an exposed card or by a sequence.

After all possible moves have been made, and vacancies filled, 10 cards are dealt from the stock face upwards to the bottom of the columns, covering the cards already in position.

Play continues in this way until the stock is exhausted. As the stock is dealt only once, the last deal from it will be of only four cards.

129

Fig. 100 Roosevelt's Favourite

The Q ♦ is built on the K ♦ and the card above it faced.
The 8 ♥ is built on the 9 ♣ and the card above it faced, the 7 ♥ is built on the 8 ♥ and the card above it faced, and the 6 ♠ is built on the 7 ♥ and the card above it faced.
Either 3 ♦ is built on the 4 ♠ and the card above it faced.
And so on.

Fig. 100

Rouge et Noir

The obvious name of *Rouge et Noir* has been given to a number of patience games. The one described here is the invention of the late Mr Charles Jewell. It is probably the best.

Deal to the board 45 cards face downwards in overlapping rows of nine cards, eight cards, seven cards, and so (dealing one card less each time) to a row of one card. The bottom card of each column is then turned face upwards (*see* Fig. 101).

The object of the game is to play any two black Aces and any two red ones to the centre as foundation-cards, and build on them ascending colour sequences to the Kings; and to build within the lay-out descending sequences of alternate colour on two black Kings to black Aces and on two red Kings to red Aces.

The face-upwards card at the foot of each column is exposed. It may be built on a foundation, packed on another exposed card in the lay-out or itself be packed on in descending sequence of alternate colour. A sequence may be moved, either as a whole or in part, from one exposed card to another, so long as the sequential order is retained. When a complete descending sequence (King to Ace) of alternate colour has been made within the lay-out it is taken out of the game, though it is not necessary to do so at once. After a card or sequence has been moved from the foot of a column the face-downwards card immediately above it is turned face upwards and becomes available for play.

A vacancy made by moving all the cards from a column

130

may be filled only by a King or by a sequence headed by a King; and it is to be noted that the game begins with a vacancy at the extreme right of the top row.

When no further moves can be made, or if the player does not wish to make further moves, he deals from the stock one card face upwards to the foot of each column, covering the card in position and filling any vacancies in the lay-out that may have been left unfilled.

The game ends when the stock has been exhausted.

It is by no means an easy game, and calls for good judgement because the player often has to choose between building a card on an Ace-foundation or on a King-foundation in the lay-out; and sometimes it is best to do neither, but to leave the card in position as a help towards clearing a column later in the game. As a complete sequence does not have to

Fig. 101 *Rouge et Noir*
The A ♣ is played to the centre and the card above it faced, the 2 ♠ is built on the A ♣ and the card above it faced.
The K ♦ is moved to fill the vacancy on the right of the 7 ♥ and the card above it faced.
The player has the option of packing either the Q ♣ or the Q ♠ on the K ♦ ; he would be advised to choose the Q ♠ as there are more face-downwards cards above it than there are above the Q ♣.
And so on.

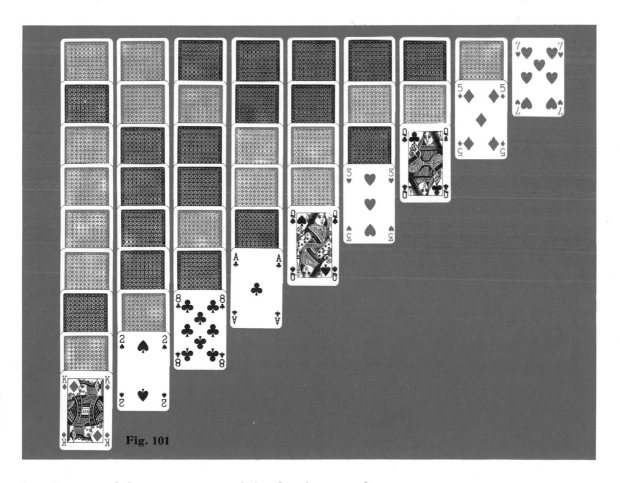

Fig. 101

be taken out of the game at once, it is often better to leave it in the game so that it may be used to release face-downwards cards in the lay-out. Every effort should be made towards shortening the length of the columns on the left-hand side of the lay-out.

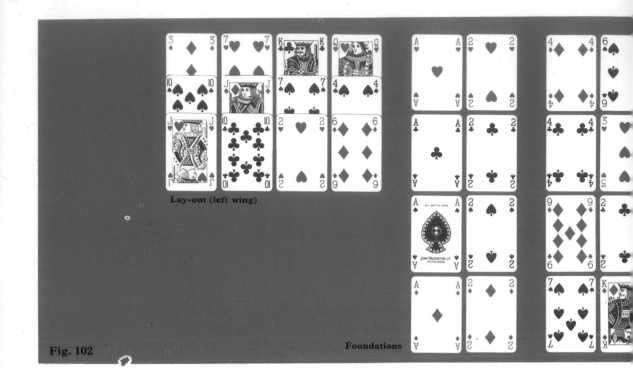

Lay-out (left wing)

Foundations

Fig. 102

Royal Cotillion

Fig. 102 Royal Cotillion
The 4 ♦ is built on the 2 ♦ and the vacancy filled.
The 6 ♦ is built on the 4 ♦, releasing the 4 ♠ that is built on the 2 ♠.
The 6 ♠ is built on the 4 ♠ and the vacancy filled, the 3 ♥ on the A ♥ and the vacancy filled, and the 3 ♣ on the A ♣ and the vacancy filled.
And so on.

Remove from the pack an Ace and a 2 from each suit, and place them face upwards in two columns – the 2s on the right of the Aces – on the centre of the board. On the left of the Aces deal face upwards 12 cards in three overlapping rows of four cards each. This is the left wing. On the right of the 2s deal face upwards 16 cards in four rows of four cards each. The rows should not overlap. This is the right wing (*see* Fig. 102).

The object of the game is, in suits, to build on the Aces in the sequence: A.3.5.7.9.J.K.2.4.6.8.10.Q. and on the 2s in the sequence: 2.4.6.8.10.Q.A.3.5.7.9.J.K.

There is no packing on the cards in the lay-out. In the left wing the bottom card of a column may be built on a foundation and the vacancy is not filled. In the right wing any card may be built on a foundation and the vacancy filled at once, either with the top card of the waste-heap or from the stock.

The stock is turned one card at a time and any card that cannot be built on a foundation nor is needed to fill a vacancy in the right wing is played to a waste-heap, the top card of which is always available to be played.

The game ends when the stock is exhausted.

132

Lay-out
(right wing)

Fig. 103 Royal Parade
The A ♦ is discarded and the 2 ♥
put in its place.
The A ♥ is discarded and the 4 ♥
put in its place.
The 7 ♥ is built on the 4 ♥, the
4 ♣ put in the place of the 7 ♥,
and the 10 ♥ built on the 7 ♥.
And so on.

Royal Parade

Royal Parade, sometimes known as Three Up, Procession, Hussars or Financier (why Financier I do not know and hesitate to hazard a guess) introduces us to the rare feature that the Aces are not wanted.

Deal face upwards to the board 24 cards in three rows of eight cards each.

The object of the game is to discard the eight Aces (they are as useless as empty bottles), move the eight 2s into the top row and build them up to the Knaves following suit by threes—2.5.8.J.; move the eight 3s into the middle row and build them up to the Queens by threes—3.6.9.Q.; and move the eight 4s into the bottom row and build them up to the Kings by threes—4.7.10.K. (*see* Fig. 103).

A foundation-card must be in its appointed row before it may be built on, and a vacancy in a row may be filled only by a foundation-card of the right rank.

When all possible moves with the originally-dealt cards have been made, eight cards are dealt face upwards in a row immediately below the lay-out. From this row all possible moves are made, and a further eight cards are then dealt from the stock to cover those cards that have not been played and to fill the vacancies left by those that have.

The game ends when the stock is exhausted and all possible moves have been made.

Fig. 103

Be on guard against losing the game by a self-block, *e.g.*
a 2 of Hearts in the top row is covered with the 5 of Hearts,
and the other 2, that is waiting for a place in the top row,
has been covered in subsequent deals by an 8 of Hearts.
When the other 8 of Hearts is dealt it should not be built on
the 5 of Hearts because, if it is, the other 2 of Hearts is
irretrievably buried and the game lost.

Fig. 104 Royal Rendezvous
The 3 ♦ is built on the A ♦ in
the lower row, the 4 ♠ on the 2 ♠
the 4 ♣ on the 2 ♣, the 6 ♣ on
the 4 ♣ and the 2 ♠ on the A ♠
in the upper row.
And so on.

Royal Rendezvous

Remove the eight Aces from the pack and a 2 of each suit.
Play the Aces to the centre in two rows of four each, and two
2s on each side of the Aces. Below them deal face upwards

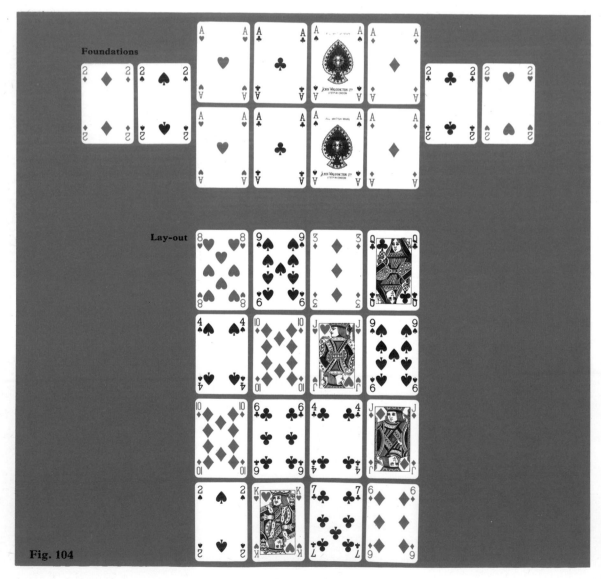

Fig. 104

134

to the board 16 cards, which may be arranged in any convenient way (*see* Fig. 104).

The object of the game is to build on the Aces in the upper row ascending suit sequences to the Kings; on the Aces in the lower row ascending suit sequences to the Kings in the order A.3.5.7.9.J.K.; and on the 2s ascending suit sequences to the Queens in the order 2.4.6.8.10.Q.

All the cards in the lay-out are available to be built on the foundation-cards, and vacancies are filled from the waste-heap, or from the stock if there is no waste-heap.

The stock is dealt one card at a time and any card that cannot be built on a foundation is played to a waste-heap, the top card of which is always available to be built on a foundation.

The game ends when the stock is exhausted.

Fig. 105(a) Saint George

The J ♥ is paired and discarded with the 3 ♦ and both vacancies are immediately filled.

The vacancy left by the 3 ♦ may be filled either with the 5 ♠ or the 2 ♣; it should be filled by the 2 ♣, which is paired and discarded with the Q ♠.

The vacancy left by the J ♥ is filled by the 9 ♦ which is paired and discarded with the 5 ♠.

The vacancy left by the Q ♠ is filled by the K ♠.

The K ♦ is paired and discarded with the A ♠ and the vacancy left by the A ♠ is filled by the 4 ♥.

The 6 ♦ is paired and discarded with the 8 ♠.

And so on.

Fig. 105(a)

135

Saint George

Deal face upwards to the board 48 cards in four squares of 12 cards each (four cards wide and three high) and arrange the four squares as a larger square with one card's width between each, forming a central cross (*see* Fig. 105(a)).

Counting the Kings as 13, the Queens as 12, the Knaves as 11 and the other cards according to the pips, the object of the game is to discard the whole pack by removing from the lay-out any two cards that together total 14 and that touch each other either at the sides, the corners or top and bottom.

When a pair of cards has been discarded from the board, the vacancies are filled by closing up the remaining cards in the row or column towards a vertical or horizontal arm of the cross, whichever the player prefers. When all discards have been made, and the rows and columns closed up, the lay-out is filled with cards from the stock (*see* Fig. 105(b)). The cards belong to the quarter to which they were dealt; the lay-out, therefore, is not closed up over the arms of the cross, though cards that touch each other—so to speak—across them are available to be discarded. It is not compulsory to discard a pair of touching cards that total 14.

The game calls for foresight and it is important to remember that the movement of the cards will be halted unless the cards in the angles of the cross are paired and discarded. Judicious pairing and discarding, coupled with skilful movement towards the arms of the cross, help to get the right card in position to discard a card from the angle of the cross where it is holding up the game.

Sometimes it is advisable not to discard a touching pair, the better play being to hold it in reserve.

The end game usually contains a number of traps into which it is easy to fall. Exact play is necessary to win the game.

Saint Helena

Saint Helena has been given the alternative names of Napoleon's Favourite and Washington's Favourite. Whether they speak the truth or not hardly matters; either way the game remains a popular one.

An Ace and a King of each suit are removed from the pack and played to the board in two rows of four cards each— the Kings above the Aces. Twelve cards are dealt face up-

Fig. 105(b)

wards to the board, so that there is a row of four cards above the Kings, a row of four cards below the Aces and a card at each end of the foundation-rows. Dealing begins above the extreme left King-foundation and continues clockwise. When 12 cards have been dealt, available cards are played (*see* Fig. 106). When all moves have been made, another 12 cards are dealt to the lay-out, covering those cards that remain in position and filling vacancies.

The object of the game is to build descending suit sequences on the Kings to the Aces and ascending suit sequences on the Aces to the Kings.

The top cards of the piles in the lay-out are available to be built on the foundations, with the restrictions that those in the row above the King-foundations may be built only on the Kings, those in the row below the Ace-foundations only

Fig. 105(b) Saint George
All possible cards have now been paired and discarded, and the rows and columns closed up.
The vacancies are now filled from the stock.

on the Aces, and those at each end of the foundation-rows on any foundation. The top cards of the piles may be built on each other either in ascending or descending sequences regardless of suit and colour; and the player may reverse the direction of a sequence on the same pile. Sequences, however, are not round-the-corner; an ascending sequence ends at a King and a descending sequence at an Ace. Only one card may be moved at a time.

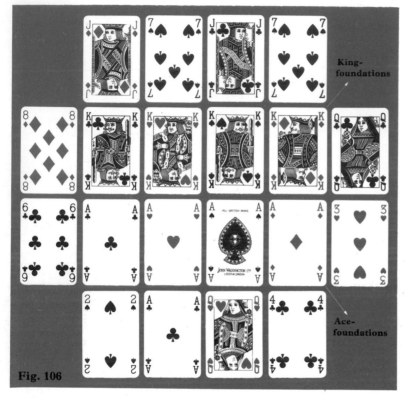

Fig. 106

Fig. 106 Saint Helena
The Q ♥ is in the wrong row to be built on the K ♥, but the Q ♣ may be built on the K ♣ and the J ♣ on the Q ♣.
The 8 ♦ is packed on either 7 ♠, the other 7 ♠ on the 8 ♦ and the 6 ♣ on the 7 ♠.
The 3 ♥ is packed on the 4 ♣.
And so on.

When the stock is exhausted a new one is formed by picking up the piles anti-clockwise, beginning with the pile at the left of the King foundation-row, and turned face downwards. Two redeals (making three deals in all) are allowed, but shuffling between them is not.

Fig. 107 Salic Law
The Ace-foundations were built up during the deal to the levels shown.
The 7 ♥ is built on the 6 ♥ and the 7 ♣ on the 6 ♦.
The 8 ♦ is built on the 7 ♥ and the 9 ♣ followed by the 10 ♣ on the 8 ♦.
The 6 ♠ is built on the 5 ♣ and the 7 ♠ on the 6 ♠.
The 9 ♦ is packed on the K ♥, the 8 ♣ is built on the 7 ♠ and the 9 ♦ on the 8 ♣.
And so on.

Salic Law

Discard the eight Queens: they play no part in the game.

Remove any King from the pack and play it to the left of the board. Deal overlapping cards, face upwards, on it until

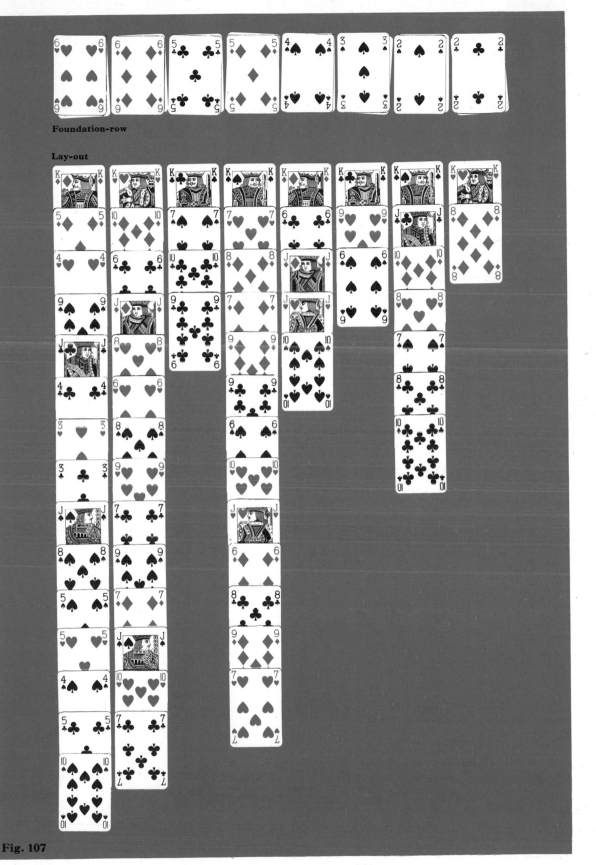

Foundation-row

Lay-out

Fig. 107

139

another King is turned up. Put this second King on the right of the first and deal cards on it. Continue to deal in this way until there are eight columns of cards, which may be of irregular length, each headed by a King.

During the deal, the Aces are played to a foundation-row immediately above the Kings. The object of the game is to build on the Aces sequences regardless of suit and colour up to the Knaves. The bottom card of a column is always available to be built on a foundation, and may be built on one while the deal is in progress (*see* Fig. 107).

When all the cards have been dealt, the play continues. The bottom cards of the columns are available to be played on the foundations. A bare King (all the cards dealt on it having been played to the foundations) is equivalent to a vacancy, and any available card may be used to fill it. The vacancy, however, may not be filled while the deal is in progress, but only after all the cards have been dealt from the stock.

The game is not such a difficult one as it may appear from the description, and the player should win one out of every three or four games. During the deal it is important to build on the foundations in such way that there will be at least one vacancy on which to begin manoeuvring when the deal has been completed. Except for this, however, the foundations should not be built too high during the deal.

The game has been given the name of Salic Law because some players, instead of discarding the Queens, play them in a row above the Aces. Played this way, if the game succeeds, the Queens will be in a row above the Knaves, in a row above the Kings—Women's Lib!

Senior Wrangler

They call it Senior Wrangler, but it involves nothing more difficult than simple arithmetic.

Suits play no part in the game: every card is taken at its pip value, the Knaves count 11, the Queens 12 and the Kings 13.

Remove from the pack eight cards from a 2 to a 9 inclusive, and place them on the board face upwards in a row. They serve as indicator-cards and take no active part in the game. After the indicator-cards have been laid out, the rest of the pack is dealt face upwards to the board in eight packets of 12 cards each, one below each indicator-card (*see* Fig. 108(a)).

Fig. 108(a)

Fig. 108(a) Senior Wrangler

The object of the game is to release eight foundation-cards, play them to the centre and build on them up to the Kings. The foundation-cards are double the value of the indicator-cards, and when a total exceeds 13 the value of the card required is found by subtracting 13 from it. Thus, the 6 of Clubs is played above the 3 of Diamonds, the Queen of Hearts above the 6 of Spades, the 5 of Diamonds above the 9 of Clubs, the 4 of Spades above the 2 of Spades and the 10 of Hearts above the 5 of Diamonds. The removal of the top card of a packet exposes the card below it (*see* Fig. 108(b)).

Fig. 108(b)

Fig. 108(b) Senior Wrangler

The sequence on each foundation-card is determined by adding the value of the foundation-card to that of the indicator-card. So after the 8 of Clubs is played above the 4 of Hearts, the Queen of Spades is built on the 8 of Clubs. The 9 of Diamonds is built on the 6 of Clubs and the 2 of Hearts on the 10 of Hearts. And so on.

When all possible moves have been made, the left-hand packet is picked up and the cards dealt in turn to the other packets. The player may deal either with the packet face upwards or face downwards, but he must deal from left to right and begin by dealing a card to the vacancy from which the packet has been taken.

The game continues in the same way, and when it comes to a halt, the packet below the 3 indicator-card is picked up and dealt.

If the game is successful, all eight foundation-cards will be built up to the Kings. If it is not, it comes to an end when all eight packets have been dealt and no further move can be made.

Fig. 109 Sly Fox
The Q ♣ is built on the K ♣ and the vacancy filled.
The Q ♦ is built on the K ♦ and the vacancy filled, and the J ♦ on the Q ♦ and the vacancy filled.
The 2 ♥ is built on the A ♥ and the vacancy filled, and the 2 ♠ on the A ♠ and the vacancy filled.
And so on.

Sly Fox

Remove an Ace and a King of each suit and play the Aces in a column to the left of the board, and the Kings in a column to the right of the board, to serve as foundations. Between the columns deal face upwards 20 cards in four rows of five cards each (*see* Fig. 109).

The object of the game is to build ascending suit sequences

Ace-foundations

King-foundations

Fig. 109

on the Aces to the Kings, and on the Kings descending suit sequences to the Aces.

There is no packing on the cards in the lay-out; they are all available, however, to be built on the foundations, and a vacancy is immediately filled by a card from the stock. When all moves have been made and the vacancies filled, cards are dealt one at a time from the stock, and any card that cannot be built on a foundation is played to cover any card in the lay-out that the player wishes. When all the cards in the lay-out have been covered, and not before they have, cards may be played from the lay-out on the foundations. The play is continued in this way until the stock is exhausted, and the game brought to an end.

Skill enters the game by playing the cards from the stock to cover those cards in the lay-out that are the less urgently needed. One card in the lay-out should be reserved for Aces and Kings and another for Queens and Knaves. Care should be taken to avoid a self-block by packing duplicate cards in opposite directions, and not in the same direction.

It is far from a difficult game, and the player who fails to win it usually has only himself to blame.

The Snake

Remove any black Ace and any red Ace from the pack and play them to the centre as foundations. As they become available the other six Aces are played in a row with them.

Deal face upwards to the board eight piles of eight cards each, and topple them forward so that all the cards may be seen (*see* Fig. 110).

The object of the game is to build ascending suit sequences on the Aces to the Kings.

The bottom cards of the columns are exposed. They may be built on the foundations, or packed on each other in descending sequences regardless of suit and colour. A sequence may be moved from one column to another, either wholly or in part, so long as the sequential order is retained. Worrying back is allowed. A vacancy made by moving all the cards of a column may be filled either with an exposed card or a sequence.

The stock is turned one card at a time, and any card that cannot be built on a foundation nor packed on the lay-out is played to the foot of the left-hand column, which becomes longer and longer and so gives the patience its name.

143

Fig. 110

Fig. 110 The Snake
The A ♣ is played to the centre.
The 10 ♦ is packed on the J ♦,
the 9 ♦ on the 10 ♦, the 8 ♣ on
the 9 ♦ and the J ♦ with the 10 ♦,
9 ♦ and 8 ♣ on the Q ♦.
The 3 ♣ is packed on the 4 ♠, and
the A ♦ is played to the centre and
the 2 ♦ built on it.
And so on.

Squadron

Deal face upwards to the board 40 cards in four over-lapping rows of 10 cards each. Put aside, face upwards, three cards to form a reserve (*see* Fig. 111).

The object of the game is to release the eight Aces, play them to the centre as foundation-cards, and build ascending suit sequences on them to the Kings.

The cards in the reserve are available to be built on the foundations, and the vacancies in the reserve filled by any exposed cards. The reserve, however, must never exceed three cards. The cards at the bottom of the columns in the lay-out are available to be built on the foundations or packed on each other in descending sequences of alternate colour. Cards may be moved only singly and not in sequences or in part-sequences. A vacancy in the lay-out, when all the cards of a column have been moved, is filled by any exposed card.

144

Fig. 111 Squadron

The 8 ♦ is packed on the 9 ♠ and the A ♥ played to the centre.

The 3 ♣ is packed on the 4 ♦, the 2 ♥ built on the A ♥ and the A ♦ played to the centre.

The 5 ♥ is packed on the 6 ♠ and the 2 ♠ on the 3 ♦.

The 7 ♣ is packed on the 8 ♦ and the A ♦ played to the centre.

The stock is dealt one card at a time, and any card that cannot be packed on the lay-out, nor built on a foundation, is played to a waste-heap, the top card of which is available to be played at all times. The game ends when the stock has been dealt once.

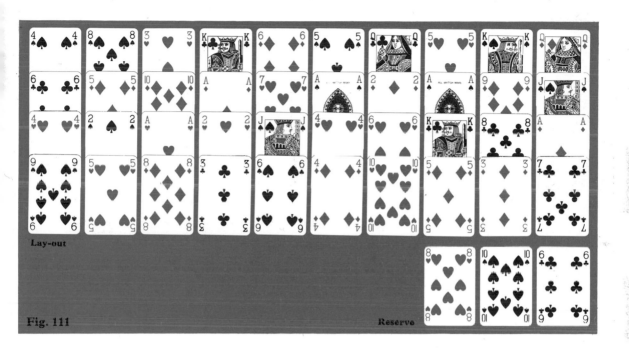

Fig. 111

Lay-out

Reserve

Steps

Deal to the board one card, below it a row of two cards, then of three cards, and so to a row of seven cards, all face downwards. Finally, a row of eight cards face upwards. For convenience the rows may overlap (*see* Fig. 112).

The object of the game is to release the eight Aces, play them to the centre as foundation-cards and build on them ascending suit sequences to the Kings.

The face-upwards cards forming the bottom row of the lay-out are available to be built on the foundations, or may be packed on each other in descending sequences of alternate colour. A sequence may be moved from one exposed card to another either as a whole or in part. When the face-upwards card at the foot of a column has been played, the face-downwards card immediately above it is turned face upwards and is available for play. A vacancy in the lay-out, when all

145

Fig. 112 Steps

The A ♣ is played to the centre.
The 4 ♥ is packed on the 5 ♣ and the J ♠ on the Q ♦.
The vacancy left by playing the J ♠ is best filled with the 6 ♠.
The face-downwards cards

released by playing the A ♣ and 4 ♥ are turned face upwards.
And so on.

Fig. 112

the cards of a column have been played, may be filled by any exposed card or sequence of cards.

The stock is turned one card at a time and any card that cannot be built on a foundation nor packed on the lay-out is played to a waste-heap, the top card of which is always available to be played.

One redeal is allowed.

Stop!

Stop!, Crapette or Russian Bank, is a competitive patience that differs from others in three ways. For one, it is a game for only two players. For another, they play their cards alternately and not simultaneously. For a third, it is governed by

146

strict rules of procedure and if a player infringes one of them his opponent may call 'Stop!' and himself take up the game.

Each player has one pack of 52 cards, which, for convenience, should be of different colour or design. The players sit opposite each other, and each deals face downwards, in a pile on his right, 12 cards, and covers it with a thirteenth face upwards. It is his depot. Alongside it he deals face upwards to the board four cards in a column; this is his file (*see* Fig. 113).

Aces, as they occur, are played between the files. They serve as foundations and are built on in ascending suit sequences to the Kings. The cards in the files are packed on in descending sequences of alternate colour. Only one card at a time may be taken from the file and built or packed elsewhere. A vacancy in the file is filled by the top card of the depot, and the card under it is turned face upwards. When all moves have been made from the file and depot, the player turns a card from his stock and if he can build it on a foundation or pack it on the file he turns the next card from his stock, and so on. His turn to play ends when a card from his stock cannot be built on a foundation nor packed on a file; the card turned from the stock is played to a waste-heap and covered with the next card of the stock turned face upwards.

The second player plays in exactly the same way, and when he has completed his moves the first player takes up the game. And so on.

A player may build on his opponent's foundations and pack on his opponent's file. He may also play cards from his depot and file (but not from his stock or waste-heap) to his opponent's waste-heap, packing it in ascending or descending sequence irrespective of suit and colour.

When a player's stock is exhausted, he picks up his waste-heap and redeals it without shuffling.

The game is won by the player who is first to get rid of all the cards in his stock and depot, by building them on the foundations or packing them on the files.

The winner scores 30 points, plus 2 points for every card remaining in the depot of his opponent, and 1 point for every card remaining in his stock and waste-heap.

The main feature of the game is the call of 'Stop!', which is made by a player if his opponent infringes any one of 10 rules of procedure. When a call of 'Stop!' is made the caller must point out which rule has been infringed and, if this is correct, the player who has called takes up the game, and begins by making as his first move the one that his opponent failed to make. A player is not compelled to call 'Stop!' if his opponent infringes a rule, but if the call is to be operative it must be made before the offender has made a further play. The rules are as follows:

1. A player must prefer to build on a foundation than pack on a file.

2. A player must prefer to pack on a file than play to his waste-heap.

3. A player must prefer to play from his depot than from his file or waste-heap.

4. A vacancy in the file must be filled before any other play is made.

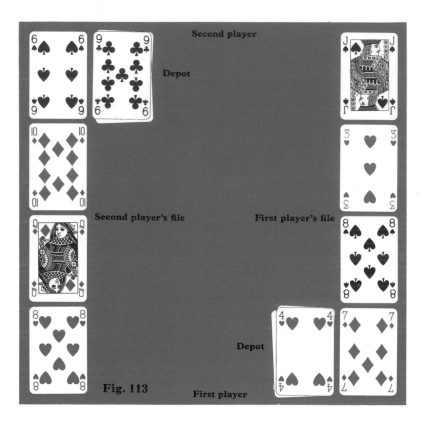

Fig. 113 Stop!

Fig. 113

5. When a card has been played from the depot, the card below it must be turned face upwards before making another play.

6. The top card of the depot must be used to fill a vacancy in the file in preference to playing it elsewhere.

7. A card in the file may be packed only in a descending sequence of alternate colour.

8. The foundation-cards can be built on only in ascending suit sequences to the Kings.

9. A player may not play a card from his opponent's file.

10. If a play is available the player must make it.

If a player calls 'Stop!' and his opponent has not infringed any of the above 10 rules, a card is transferred from the player's depot to that of the player who called.

Sultan (of Turkey)

Remove from the pack one Ace of Hearts and the eight Kings. Place a King of Hearts on the centre of the board and a King on each side of it. Place three Kings in a row below

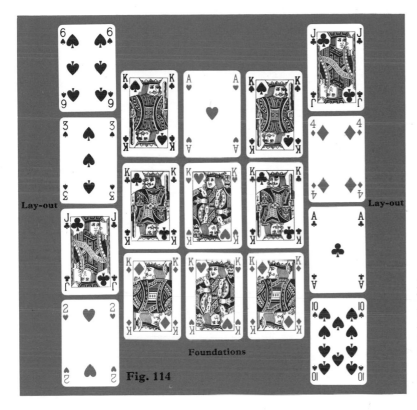

Foundations

Fig. 114

Fig. 114 Sultan (of Turkey)
The 2 ♥ is built on the A ♥, and the A ♣ on either K ♣.
As yet, there is no waste-heap, and the vacancies may be filled from the stock: it is, however, better to leave them unfilled until a waste-heap is begun and a choice of two cards can be made.

them, and the Ace of Hearts above the central King of Hearts with a King on each side of it. On each side of the lay-out deal face upwards a column of four cards (*see* Fig. 114).

The object of the game is to build an ascending suit sequence on the Ace of Hearts to the Queen, and on the Kings (with the exception of the central King of Hearts) ascending suit sequences to the Queens.

The cards in the two columns are available to be built on the Ace of Hearts and the Kings; they must not be packed on other cards in the columns nor themselves be packed on. A vacancy in a column may be filled with a card either from the waste-heap or the stock.

The stock is dealt one card at a time and cards that cannot

149

be built on the Ace of Hearts or King-foundations are played to a waste-heap, the top card of which is available to be played.

Two redeals are allowed.

Skill enters the game in the management of the columns –when to leave a vacancy unfilled, and which card to choose for filling one.

If the game succeeds the central King of Hearts (the Sultan) will be surrounded by the eight Queens (his harem). The game has been given the alternative name of the Emperor of Germany; it is hardly in the best of taste.

Switch-back

Discard the eight Kings. They are not wanted.

Remove one Ace of each suit and place them in a square in the centre of the board, to serve as foundations. Deal face upwards 12 cards around them in a çircle (*see* Fig. 115).

The object of the game is to build suit sequences on the Aces in the impertinent order: A.2.3.4.5.6.Q.J.10.9.8.7. and then, in reverse, 7.8.9.10.J.Q.6.5.4.3.2.A.

Fig. 115 Switch-back
The 2 ♠ is built on the A ♠ and the 3 ♠ on the 2 ♠.
The vacancies are filled from the stock, because, as yet, there are no waste-heaps.
And so on.

Foundations

Fig. 115

150

The cards in the circle may be built on the foundations and the vacancies filled either from the stock or from one of the waste-heaps.

The stock is dealt one card at a time, and any that cannot be built on a foundation is played to one of four waste-heaps, at the discretion of the player.

The stock is dealt only once, but the player has the grace of shuffling each waste-heap once.

Success depends very largely on how the player distributes the cards among the waste-heaps. It is, however, not such a difficult game as it may seem, because at every turn of a card there are 17 cards to choose from—12 in the circle, the four top cards of the waste-heaps and the top card of the stock.

Teenagers

Remove from the pack a Queen of Hearts and a Knave of Hearts and play them to the centre as foundations. As they become available play to the centre the two 10s of Spades, 10s of Diamonds and 10s of Clubs.

Fig. 116 Teenagers
Play the 10 ♣ to the centre.
Build the 9 ♣ on the 10 ♣, the K ♥ on the Q ♥ and the A ♥ on the K ♥.
Another 16 cards are dealt from the stock, to cover the cards left in position in the lay-out and fill the vacancies left by the 10 ♣, 9 ♣, K ♥ and A ♥.
And so on.

Fig. 116

The object of the game is to build on the Queen of Hearts an ascending, round-the-corner suit sequence to the Knave, on the Knave of Hearts a descending, round-the-corner suit sequence to the Queen, and on the six 10s descending, round-the-corner suit sequences to the Knaves. It will be seen that if the game is successful a Queen of Hearts will be

151

accompanied by seven Knaves, which accounts for the name of the game.

Deal face upwards to the board 16 cards in two rows of eight cards each (*see* Fig. 116). The cards are available to be built on the foundations, and when all moves have been made, another 16 cards are dealt from the stock to cover those in position and to fill any vacancies that may have been made by playing cards from the lay-out to the foundations.

The play is continued in this way until the stock is exhausted. After this, whenever play comes to a standstill, each pile in the lay-out is picked up in turn and dealt to the lay-out, beginning with a card to the vacancy from which the pile has been taken.

The game ends when all 16 piles have been dealt, unless, of course, success comes first.

Toad (in the Hole)

Faute de mieux, let the name stand. It is as good as any and the alternative name of Frog is no better.

Deal a pile of 13 cards and place it to the left of the board as a heel. If any Aces are dealt, play them to a foundation-row and bring the heel up to 13 cards. If no Aces are dealt, remove one from the pack and play it as a foundation.

Fig. 117 Toad (in the Hole)

Fig. 117

The object of the game is to build on the eight Aces ascending sequences to the Kings regardless of suit and colour. The stock is dealt one card at a time and any card

152

that cannot be played to a foundation is played to one or other of five waste-heaps, at the choice of the player. The top cards of the waste-heaps and the top card of the heel are available to be played to the foundations (*see* Fig. 117). The stock is dealt only once.

Success at the game largely depends on good management of the waste-heaps. One should be reserved for Kings and Queens. On the other four it is usually best to pack them, as far as it is possible to do so, in descending sequences. It is unwise to put too many cards of the same rank on the same waste-heap.

Travellers

Deal to the board, face downwards in a row, eight piles of 13 cards each. Turn the top card of each pile face upwards and play them to the centre in a row to serve as foundations (*see* Fig. 118).

The object of the game is to build ascending, round-the-corner sequences, irrespective of suit and colour, of 13 cards each on the eight foundation-cards.

The eight piles are turned face upwards and the top card of each is exposed and available to be built on a foundation. When the top card of a pile has been played, the card under it becomes available.

When all moves have been made, the left-hand pile is picked up and dealt, one card at a time, face upwards to the piles, beginning with the vacancy from which the pile has been taken and filling any vacancies that may have been made

Fig. 118 Travellers
Build the Q ♥ on the J ♠ and the K ♥ on the Q ♦, Q ♥ or Q ♠.
Build the A ♠ on the K ♥, the 7 ♥ or 7 ♦ on the 6 ♦, the 8 ♥ on the 7 and the 6 ♣ on either the 5 ♥ or 5 ♠.
And so on.

Fig. 118

by all the cards of a pile having been built on a foundation.

The game ends, unless it is won first, when every pile has been dealt once.

Triple Line

Triple Line is a classic example of a building-up patience; this need not be held against it, however, because it is a fascinating one to play.

Deal face upwards to the board 36 cards in three overlapping rows of 12 cards each. Aces, as they become available, are played to the centre as foundation-cards, to be built on in ascending suit sequences to the Kings (*see* Fig. 119).

The cards at the bottom of the columns are available to be built on the foundations, or packed on each other in descending sequences of alternate colour. Provided the sequential order and alternation of colour is retained, a sequence may be moved from the foot of one column to that of another, either as a whole or in part. A vacancy in the lay-out, made when all the cards of a column have been played, may be filled by an exposed card or by a sequence.

Fig. 119 Triple Line

The A ♠ is played to the centre. The 7 ♦ is packed on the 8 ♣ and the A ♦ played to the centre. The 6 ♠ is packed on the 7 ♦ and the 2 ♦ built on the A ♦. The 5 ♣ is packed on the 6 ♥ and the A ♠ played to the centre. The 5 ♦ is packed on the 6 ♠, the J ♣ on the Q ♥, the 10 ♦ on the J ♣ and the 8 ♠ on the 9 ♥. The vacancy is filled by the 8 ♣ with the 7 ♦, 6 ♠ and 5 ♦. And so on.

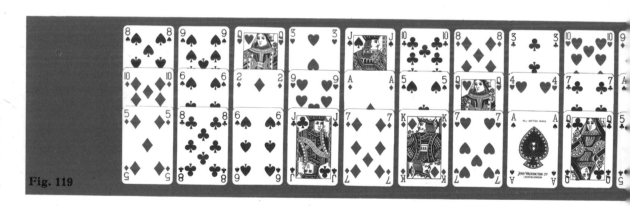

Fig. 119

The stock is dealt one card at a time and any that cannot be built on a foundation nor packed on the lay-out is played to a waste-heap, the top card of which is always available to be played. One redeal is allowed.

Virginibus Puerisque

Deal face upwards to the board 25 cards in five rows of five cards each. Counting the Kings as 13, the Queens as 12 and the Knaves as 11, remove from the board any pairs of cards

Fig. 120 *Virginibus Puerisque*
The Q ♦ is discarded with the
2 ♣, the 10 ♥ with the 4 ♠, the
8 ♦ with the 6 ♦, the K ♦ with
the A ♥ and the 7 ♠ with the
7 ♣.
And so on.

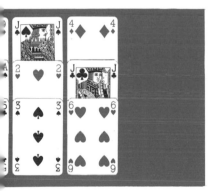

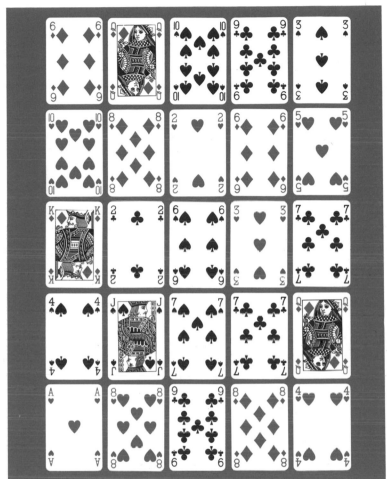

Fig. 120

in the same row or column that total 14 (*see* Fig. 120).

The object of the game is to discard in this way the whole pack.

When no more discards can be made, the vacancies are filled by cards dealt from the stock, beginning at the extreme left of the top row. If cards remain on the board after the stock is exhausted, the lowest row is taken up and dealt to fill the vacancies from left to right; if cards still remain on the board, another row is taken up, and so on. If at any time the game comes to a standstill, and the stock has not been exhausted, the player may alter the position of any two cards in the lay-out.

Windmill

Windmill, or Propeller, is a fairly easy game with a simple lay-out.

Play to the centre of the board any one King. Deal face upwards two cards in a column above it and two below it, and two in a row on both sides of it (*see* Fig. 121). As they become available, play to the four angles the first four Aces

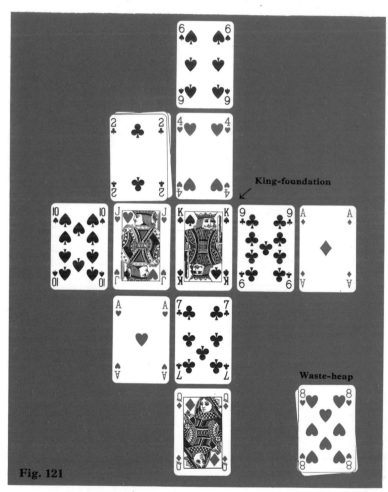

Fig. 121 Windmill
The A ♦ is played to either vacant angle.
The Q ♦ is built on the K ♠.
The 8 ♥ should be chosen to fill one of the vacancies, because good play dictates holding in the lay-out as many cards of different rank as is possible.
And so on.

Fig. 121

that are dealt either in the lay-out or from the stock.

The object of the game is to build on the central King a descending, round-the-corner sequence of 52 cards, regardless of suit and colour, and ascending sequences, regardless of suit and colour, on the four Aces to the Kings.

The top card of the waste-heap and the eight cards of the lay-out are available to be built on the foundations, and at any time the top card of an Ace-foundation may be built on

156

the central King-foundation, but only one card may be so taken from each Ace-foundation.

A vacancy in the lay-out must be filled at once either from the stock or by the top card of the waste-heap.

The stock is dealt one card at a time. When it is exhausted, the waste-heap is turned face downwards and dealt. Play continues but only for as long as a card dealt from the waste-heap can be played to a foundation.

Definitions

Available card—A card that may be played in such way as the rules of the game permit.

Blocked—A card so situated that it cannot be moved without infringing the rules of the game.

Board—The flat surface on which the game is played.

Build—To place a card on a foundation-card in such order as the rules of the game dictate.

Centre—The unoccupied part of the board above the layout.

Column—Two or more cards placed perpendicularly on the board, one immediately below the other, or slightly overlapping each other for convenience.

Exposed card—A card at the bottom of a column, extreme right of a fan, or the top of a foundation-pile or waste-heap, which may be played on, or moved, subject to the rules of the game.

Fan—Two or more cards arranged on the board in open formation, like a fan.

Foundation-card—A card played to the centre, and on which a complete suit or sequence has to be built in accordance with the rules of the game.

Foundation-pile—The cards built on the foundation-card in accordance with the rules of the game.

Foundation-row—The foundation-cards arranged in a row in the centre.

Grace—The privilege limited to some games of making an illegal move.

Heel—A number of cards counted out at the beginning of the game and placed apart to be used as directed by the rules of the game.

158

Lay-out–The cards laid out on the board in a prescribed pattern to be moved or packed on in accordance with the rules of the game.

Pack–To place a card on one exposed in the lay-out in such order as the rules of the game dictate.

Row–Two or more cards placed horizontally on the board, side by side, or slightly overlapping each other for convenience.

Sequence–Two or more cards following one another in correct order, but not necessarily of the same suit.

Sequence, Ascending–A sequence progressing from low to high (*e.g.* Acc . . . King).

Sequence, Descending–A sequence progressing from high to low (*e.g.* King . . . Acc).

Sequence, Round the-corner–A sequence in which the highest card is considered adjacent to the lowest (*e.g.* . . . 3.2.A.K.Q . . . or . . . Q.K.A.2.3 . . .).

Sequence, Suit– A sequence in which all the cards are of the same suit.

Stock–The undealt cards of the pack which may be used later in the game.

Vacancy–An unoccupied space in the lay-out.

Waive–The privilege limited to some games of lifting a card in order to play the one underneath it.

Waste-heap–The pile of cards consisting of those that could not be played either to a foundation-pile or to an exposed card in the lay-out.

Worry-back–The privilege limited to some games of returning cards from the foundation-piles to the lay-out.